Skyline
2018

Cyberworld Publishing

www.CyberworldPublishing.com

Cyberworld Publishing
Toronto, NSW, 2283
Australia

Skyline
2018

*An Anthology of
Prose and Poetry by
Central Virginia Writers*

Olivia Stowe, ed.

Table of Contents

Poetry

Prose Nonfiction

On Writing/Publishing

Introduction

Skyline 2018, the fifth in a series of annual publisher's anthologies produced by Cyberworld Publishing, showcases the prose and poetry talents of writers who live or work in Central Virginia or otherwise have writing connections to the region. The title of the anthology is taken from the Skyline Drive, the parkway skipping along the top of the Blue Ridge Mountains in Virginia and providing centering for the region to which the authors showcased here are connected. The first four editions followed the seasons in cover image and *Skyline* contest themes. The theme for this, fifth, edition and this year's annual *Skyline* writing contest is "nighttime on the mountain."

Other than the 2017 *Skyline* contest "nighttime on the mountain" theme, which some invited authors and poets have also adopted as the setting of their pieces, there is no overarching theme for the short stories, poems, and essays in this anthology, however, so each can be discovered and appreciated on its own context and merits. Eclectic is the hallmark word for this collection. Nearly half of the works found here won or placed in various Virginia regional and statewide writing contests between September 2016 and September 2017. The foundation for the juried contest selections combine the 2017 *Skyline* writing contest and the 2017 contest of the Blue Ridge Writers Chapter (BWRC) of the Virginia Writers Club (VWC). Selected contest-placing works from the 2016 poetry awards of the Poetry Society of Virginia; a first-placed poem in the 2016 Writer's Eye contest, sponsored by the Fralin Museum of the University of Virginia; and the winning poetry poem in the 2017 Appalachian Writers Guild chapter of the VWC are also published here.

Also included in the anthology are two works by the *Skyline* and BWRC contests coordinator Gary D. Kessler, works by contest judges Sarah Collins Honenberger (both *Skyline* and BWRC contests judge for fiction) and Stephen Bush (anthology publisher and BWRC contest judge for nonfiction), and a short story by *Skyline* volume editor Olivia Stowe. Other contest judges included Liz Dixon (both *Skyline* and BWRC contests judge for poetry) and Becky Mushko (*Skyline* contest judge for nonfiction). All are established writers and all have helped in selection and publication of earlier editions of the anthology. Additional works include pieces selected by the judges from the portfolios of the contest entrants and special contributor works by established writers in the Central Virginia region.

The anthology is made up of fifty-five works by twenty-seven authors, presented in four sections: fiction (fourteen short stories), poetry (twenty-nine poems), nonfiction (eight essays), and, since this is a writer's anthology, a section on writing and publishing (three essays and one poem). Nearly half of the authors here are represented by more than one work and in varied media to showcase their writing skills.

Each edition of *Skyline* has lifted a featured writer or poet for recognition in addition to the works of invited established authors and contest judges, which are placed at the top of category sections. *Skyline 2018* features and celebrates three male poets: Stanley A. Galloway, David Black, and Jack Trammell.

A notable additional section to this anthology is the "About the Authors" section, which provides fascinating, I think, literary background notes on the authors connected with the Central Virginia region and represented in this collection.

As with the four earlier annual *Skyline* editions, it has been a delight to work with and discover the many varied themes and high quality of writing of these Central Virginia writers. I hope you will find these works as fresh and as entertaining and thought provoking as I have. These indeed are exceptional writers who deserve to have their works highlighted and represented in the marketplace.

Olivia Stowe
Volume Editor
Skyline 2018

PROSE FICTION

A Trip to Abilene

Jody Hobbs Hesler

The day your daddy kidnaps you, you go to the curbside like you would at the end of any other school day. You don't see Alice's car waiting there, so you head toward the bench to wait. Alice takes you home from school every day and keeps you at her apartment until your mother is finished with work. But sometimes Alice is late. She has her other job, the one where she takes care of the old people at the nursing home. When she runs late, she wants you to just wait for her on the bench. She says kindergartners are old enough to wait as long as they don't talk to strangers.

From the bench by the playground, you recognize the car pulling up to the curb. It's your daddy's car, the new one. He's sitting behind the wheel. When he sees you, he waves. He lives far away and you only see him on weekends. Today is Wednesday. You remember how he acts funny when you come to visit and don't look happy to see him. His house is supposed to feel like your house. So you smile and try not to look surprised.

"Let's go, Abigail," your daddy says. "Get in the car."

"Where's Alice?" you ask. You stay on the sidewalk, holding your bookbag.

"I don't know about Alice," your daddy says. "But your mom's in the hospital. You have to come with me today."

"Are we going to your house? Do we need to get my things?" You wait on the sidewalk.

"I've got everything you need," your daddy says, but you don't see any of your things in the car. Your daddy's face has a funny look on it. You don't want to make him angry. You open the back door, slide in, and buckle your seat belt. Your daddy drives the car away from the curb.

You look around the backseat and on the floor for your favorite toy. "Did you bring Lambie?"

"No," your daddy says.

You look around again anyway. "Are we going somewhere overnight?"

"Yes, your mom's in the hospital. We're going away overnight."

Lambie always comes with you on trips. You can't sleep without Lambie. "For how long?"

"Christ, Abigail. How the hell should I know?" Your daddy casts a quick look toward you in the backseat. Sweat stands out on his upper lip in little clear beads. "A few nights at least."

Your daddy drives for a long time. "I need to pee," you say. The school bathrooms smell like Granny Tay-Tay's basement when it floods. You always wait to pee until the end of the school day.

"We'll be there soon," he says. But the road keeps running past you.

Your mother must have gotten sick awfully fast. She was happy at breakfast this morning. You remember the regular waking-up look on her face when she poured your orange juice.

Your stomach aches from needing to pee. You're hungry, too. Alice always gives you a muffin and some fruit, maybe a glass of milk, right after school. "I'm hungry."

"Not now," your daddy says. But a few minutes later he pulls into a parking lot at a donut store. "Don't dilly dally," he says. "We're in a hurry." You walk inside, then run to the bathroom. When you come back out to the donut counter, Daddy stuffs a bag into your hands. He pushes one of his hands into your back, leading you toward the car. All the while, he looks side to side in the store and in the parking lot, like he's looking for something.

"You all right, Daddy?"

"Why wouldn't I be all right?" he says. "Just hurry up." He scoots you into the car and doesn't notice how the door scrapes your arm on your way in.

In the car, you pull out two donuts and a carton of milk. You hold the milk container against the sting of the scrape to cool it. Your daddy forgot to pack a straw or any napkins, but all you're thinking is how Alice would never give donuts as a snack. Your mouth waters. You eat both donuts and use the waxy wrapping from them to try to get the sticky feeling off your fingers. You pour the milk from the spout straight into your mouth. Only a little spills. The waxy paper doesn't help to get it off the seat of your daddy's new car. You use your sock for that.

Donuts make a cool snack, but then you start feeling sick. It's way past supper now. The sun is dark orange at the edge of the sky. "Are we going to your house? Isn't this too far?"

"Don't be a smart aleck," your daddy says. But you weren't trying to be a smart aleck, so you get confused. You're thinking Alice could've taken care of you just fine. If Alice was taking care of you, you'd be in your own bed right now, hugging Lambie. When Alice sits for you at night, she likes to hum a bedtime tune, which is very thin and sweet. Why does your daddy need to pick you up?

Maybe it's because your mommy is very, very sick. And you begin to think of all the things that could be wrong with her, all the different kinds of sicknesses you've heard of. The insides of your stomach tighten and hurt. "Daddy, I'm going to be sick." But he doesn't want to stop. You can't help it—you throw up in the backseat.

"Jesus, Abigail," your father says. But he keeps driving. So you start to cry. "There's nowhere to stop," he says, and he looks at you with helpless-looking eyes and the sunset behind him.

Through the window, you watch the side of the road fly past. To you, every bit of the side of the road looks like a good place to stop. Somehow you keep yourself from throwing up again. You roll down the window and stick your nose out of the car, like a dog, to cut the smell.

"What's wrong with Mommy?"

"Nothing," your daddy says. "She just had to go to the hospital. She can't take care of you for a while."

"But will she be okay? When can I see her? Why are we going away from her when she's sick?" When you're sick, your mother takes off work and sits beside your bed. You play cards together, and you drink juice with ice cubes.

"She needed a break, all right? A break from taking care of you. You're a lot of work. Look at you, with all that puke in

17

the backseat. A lot of work," your daddy says. You don't want to be a lot of work. You try to wipe the throw up into the donut bag with the waxy paper. "What the hell are you doing?" your daddy asks.

"Cleaning up," you say.

"Well, don't."

Your eyes start crusting over from being tired. You see a sign outside the car window, lit up in the headlights, that says, "Welcome to Abilene." You like it because it sounds like your name and because you like to read new words.

Your daddy pulls over at a roadside motel. You hear him ask the clerk how far it is to Mexico. The clerk says just a few more hours and hands your daddy a key. He asks for extra towels. Once he puts you in the hotel room, he tells you, "Clean yourself up. Take a shower."

"I don't know how," you say, because you only take baths and your mother always fixes the temperature first. She always warns you about hot water.

All your daddy says is, "You'll figure it out." Then he takes a bunch of the extra hotel towels out to the car to use for cleaning up the backseat. He stays out there a long time, and you don't figure out how to start the shower.

You feel gross after throwing up and only eating donuts for hours and hours. You think about calling your house, even though no one could be there with Mommy at the hospital. Still, you like the idea of the phone ringing back at home.

When you're at home, you can hear the phone from your room. You picture your room—nighttime out your window and Lambie sitting where you left him on your pillow. You wish you were there. So you decide to place a collect call the way your mommy taught you to, right after Daddy moved out, so it would always be okay for you to call home.

You expect the phone to ring and ring. You think it will make you feel good, knowing the phone is ringing back where you would like to be and where you would hear it. You are really surprised when someone picks up the phone after the very first ring. Your mother accepts the charges. She doesn't hear you asking, "What are you doing home?" She's too busy saying, "Thank, God, Abigail!" and "Where are you, sweetie? Are you okay?"

You tell her, "I'm okay. But I threw up. I had donuts for supper, and I don't feel too good."

"Where are you, then, sweetie?" Your mommy's voice sounds afraid, and you aren't sure why. Your mother's the one who's sick, so you're the one who should be scared.

"Why are you home, Mommy? I thought you were in the hospital."

Then your mother sounds calm all of a sudden, and like she's acting something out. "It's okay, Abigail. I'm fine. I'm not in the hospital." There must be something you don't understand right. This is how grown-ups act when there's something the kid doesn't know about. "Why would you think I was in the hospital?" your mommy asks.

"Daddy said."

"Is Daddy with you?"

"He's outside cleaning the throw up out of his car."

"Where are you, honey?"

"We went through a town called Abilene," you say. "I noticed it because it looked like Abigail on the sign."

"That's great, sweetheart. That's good reading. Where are you calling from now?"

"A hotel," you say. "A hotel with a giant swan on a sign outside it. It's the Swan Inn, I think." Something is wrong. You can tell. You feel afraid in your body, your throat and your stomach. "I'm not supposed to be here, am I, Mommy?" But she doesn't answer that.

"Just stay put, honey. Whatever you do, in the morning, try not to leave the room. And don't tell your Daddy you called me, okay?"

Now you hear his footsteps outside. So you hang up the phone really fast and head into the bathroom. You turn on the cold water in the bathtub so it's running when your daddy opens the hotel room door. You're afraid to add any hot water. You wash your hands and face, and you wash off your clothes a little, too. You're not supposed to be here, so you're not sure what to do. You're not sure how long you need to stay in the bathroom before your daddy will think you're finished. You stay in there until he knocks.

"Stop looking at me with those bug eyes, Abigail," your daddy says when you come back out. You didn't know you had bug eyes. "Go to bed," he says. Then he lies down and soon starts snoring. He doesn't even turn off the light.

For a while, you sit up at the window, watching cars going by and some going in and out of the parking lot. The covers on the bed smell bad, like cigarettes. The light in the ceiling makes a humming noise. Your clothes are still wet from where you tried to clean them. You hear a few people walking down along the walkway outside the room. Late into the night, the people walking by use loud voices and sound strange.

All the while, you're thinking if you keep sitting here, your mommy will come get you and take you back to where you're supposed to be. You don't like doing something wrong.

When the sun starts to lighten the sky, you wonder why it is taking your mommy so long to come get you. Before your daddy wakes up, you go into the bathroom and lock the door. That way you're sure you won't have to leave before your mommy comes for you.

But your daddy wakes up and needs to pee. He starts banging on the door. You don't say anything. You pretend to be asleep. Your father keeps saying he'll rip the door down. But you figure out how somebody would hear that for sure, and then he'd get caught, because you aren't supposed to be here, and he's doing something wrong.

So you stay in there. Your daddy doesn't even pound the door very hard. You figure you'll be safe this way for a little while, even though your throat feels tight and you're hungry and afraid.

After a while, your mommy will come, and she'll take you wherever it is you're supposed to be. She'll bring some cereal and milk for you, and she'll comb the tangles out of your hair. She'll buy some toothpaste so you can brush the sour throw up taste out of your mouth. Meanwhile, you hug your knees to your chest and listen to your daddy's pounding. You rock back and forth.

The sound of the pounding blurs with another sound. It takes a few minutes before you can tell that someone has started knocking outside on the hotel room door. You feel relieved because you're sure it's your mother at last.

But it turns out to be police. You hear them breaking through the hotel room door, and then you hear your daddy saying something about how there's nothing to worry about. But the police officers don't believe him and they tell him to open the bathroom door. "It's locked," he says.

"Who's in there?" they ask. He doesn't say anything. Someone starts pulling on the bathroom doorknob, and somebody else says, "Bradley William Temple, you are under arrest . . . you have the right to remain silent . . ." Just like on TV.

You hear a click, and you're sure somebody put handcuffs on your father. In a minute, a police officer tears the locked bathroom door clear off its hinges. Then he kneels down on the floor beside you. In the background, your daddy stands with his hands bound behind him. A police officer holds one of his arms. He's trying to get you to look at him. You are trying not to look.

"You seem pretty shook up," your officer says. You don't answer. "I'm going to take you to your mommy," he says. "Come on out to the car with me. We'll go down to the station."

"No," you say. "I want my mommy to come here." Your officer trades looks with the one who's holding your daddy's arm. You think they will put handcuffs on you, too. You think they will arrest you because you won't go with them and because you're not supposed to be here. But you keep saying, "Mommy said to wait for her." Then you rock and rock and say mommy over and over.

Your officer sits down beside you. "Okay then," he says in a soft voice. "How about if I sit here with you until your mommy comes. How about that?" You nod. "Hey, Ben," your officer shouts to the one taking your daddy away.

Your daddy cuts in. "Don't believe them, Abigail. We were going to be just fine. Don't believe them. Whatever they tell you."

Ben, the one holding your daddy, yanks him extra hard to get him out the door. You think it probably hurt him. You know your daddy must be scared in handcuffs. Also you don't want him to know that you are less afraid now that he is being taken away. So you tell him, "It's okay, Daddy."

Then your officer says, "Ben," again, and then, "Send us up some bagels and a banana or something, okay?"

You hear the shuffling noises of the police officer taking your daddy out of the room and down the walkway outside. Your daddy argues and whines like a dog. Then for a few minutes you hear your officer's walkie talkie coughing and some voices on there saying words and numbers you don't understand. Then it's mostly quiet.

When the food comes back with another police officer, yours puts cream cheese on a bagel. He cuts it in half and in half again so the pieces are small and easy to hold. He opens the milk and helps you with the straw. He peels the banana. He hands you each thing saying, "There you go. You're going to be okay." But you can see behind his eyes, which are brown and very nice, that he isn't sure about that at all.

Son of Crown of Thorns

Sarah Collins Honenberger

Vandy doesn't lasso steers or hang a six gun off his belt. But he knows there are places west of here—far west of Virginia—where guys his age walk bowlegged and feel the world move under their thighs, places where they dream about bucking broncos even in their sleep, where sitting a bull is like turning in bottles for the deposit money, a natural part of life.

"D'you have the entry fee?" Calvin asks, quietly, so as not to wake the bulls that stand slumped, tails switching, eyes half-closed. Like the cowboys who wander back and forth with the same lowered eyes and leaden feet, the bulls hold their eagerness for the competition secretly in check.

Vandy turns up the sky-blue cuff on his yellow plaid shirt and tweaks the collar. It's stiff and warm from hanging from the gun rack inside the truck since he ironed it this morning before work. He shakes his head at his friend. "That's like the fifth time you asked about the effing entry fee."

Calvin stands his ground.

Vandy glares. "I said I had the money, didn't I?"

"Just checking. We come this far for eight lousy seconds, two and a half GD hours in your stinking truck after working all day, I wanna be sure you're not just pissing in a puddle."

"I come to ride." Vandy toes the heel on his right boot, loosening it enough to pull it off while standing. Hopping on the other boot, he grabs the handle of the nylon duffle and works the zipper. Two red boots fall out, flared at the top, trimmed in canary yellow. He smudges his thumb across the feathery design of cactus flower tufts to wipe the dust. They cost him a month's salary, but he'd never admit that to anyone.

Calvin jabs at the tooled leather and hooks the other boot with one finger. It spins before it drops again. "Dancing shoes? Didn't take you for a queen."

Vandy plants his bare foot in the dust and aims one fist at Calvin's stomach. His other hand reaches down and retrieves the boot. As Calvin feigns injury, his knees buckled, his arms

23

wrapped around his middle, he pretends to choke and spits into the dust. A tiny puddle of saliva sits on the gray powder. Desire and reality, the bottom line.

Vandy knows he should laugh. Hitting anyone would be a mistake. His broken ribs from two weeks ago haven't fully healed. They're taped, but if—when—the bull bucks and twists, his ribcage will twist too. Added to whatever he might have done to his hand by throwing the punch. Stupid, when he's so close to qualifying for Nationals.

He sinks back against the light post to put on the boots. Along the metal farm gates a dozen bags almost identical to his lie abandoned. Those gates lace together temporary pens for the bulls, ominously still, vociferously silent. Cowboys lounge along the rails. They strap on chaps, switch out the everyday for show boots, or finger tobacco to parsed lips. Muffled murmurs, no conversations. One or two look in the direction of the stands, where the crowd fills in from the top row down. Across the metal planks hats bob and children wriggle. Girls thumb their camisole straps. Mothers spread out newspapers to save space on the bleachers. To the cowboys, spectators are insignificant, no matter what the event sponsors say about attendance and profits.

While Calvin moans, play-acting, his head still on his knees, Vandy rummages in the bag. After he locates two small leather straps, he tightens one around each of his calves about halfway up the boot. When he straightens, his shoulders arch back with the swagger of an enlisted man whose sweetheart is waving him good-bye.

"I'm gonna sign in," Calvin says. "You change your mind?"

"Hell, no," Vandy barks, but he doesn't follow right away.

Halfway down the rails a stocky fellow in a black Stetson and faded black jeans stands bowlegged on the platform. He fiddles with the microphone, his eyes glued to the list of names on his clipboard. His broadcast voice wavers in the open air like a last-minute vulture above the tarmac. When the announcer calls the first competitor, Vandy recognizes the name of a bull rider who's been to Nationals every year for the last six. His stomach flips. The odds go up.

As the cowboy settles onto the bull, the announcer speaks sideways, chatty and grinning. "Why, lookee here, a familiar face on tonight's list. Vandy Sodern, back again? You just can't stay away. Even after that bull et your earlobe last week." He pauses for the crowd's laughter. "You look for a paycheck tonight, Sodern?"

The spotlight swings over the field and finds Vandy. "Farley." Vandy strings the curse words together under his breath. "Don't you be talking at me about paychecks. You ain't never had a Saturday night date in your life."

"Date? You know I can't do fruit."

They've all heard the joke before. It isn't worth a full-blown laugh, but Vandy smiles anyway, partly because he knows the crowd is watching, mostly because Farley sometimes judges the first round if they're short on officials. There's no point in pissing him off. A date, who is he kidding? The last date he can remember is a church picnic when he was still living at home two, maybe three years ago. Somebody's little sister was the setup. Vandy's father offered the girl his half-empty long-neck after a swipe with his shirttail and then called Vandy names when he steered the girl away before the old man could substitute her for the bottle. Not much of a threat, the old man did his usual and passed out before dinner. But the insult remains, as if the girl couldn't possibly be interested in a wannabe cowboy.

Once the girl saw the tarmac through the floorboard in Vandy's ancient truck, she cut out for home with school friends. The bull riding circuit doesn't leave much time or money for dating. Or vehicles.

By the time the overhead speakers burst into a high-pitched "Star-Spangled Banner," Vandy and Calvin are clothes-pinned to the fence, helping the second rider sit the bull. Vandy can hear the other cowboys muttering curses and prayers to themselves and love songs to the watery-eyed bulls wedged against the two breakaway gates on either side of the six-foot digital timer. It's all show for the crowds. Anyone here for the first time will be thinking eight seconds, how hard could that be? The bulls look sleepy. And the cowboys strut about as if they've been counting to eight since the day they were born.

Twelve cowboys later—only one past five seconds and all twisting off the bulls in double time to clear the flailing hooves—the loudspeaker announces Calvin's name and his bull, Little Yellow Jacket.

"A ringer," says Rick, older and wiser, with taped hands that look like department store white gloves.

"More like a stinger," Vandy shoots back. No one pokes fun at his friend and gets away with it. He knows the bull's lineage. They all do. Besides, on any given night the bull you draw is only half the challenge. How much Wild Turkey you consumed the night before, whether you have sponsors watching, which girl has paid admission to see you perform. Hell, the bull doesn't know the man on his back hocked his truck to meet the entry fee. The bull won't know the cowboy is halfway to Nationals and wants that Vegas chance more than he's ever wanted any woman. But the rider knows it, and that makes the eight seconds longer than most men can stand.

Calvin leans forward, his knees clenched against the bull's gut, his hand wrapped in the rosined leather, the tail rope taut. Eyes wide, he sits back and flings his free hand into the air, the signal for the gate crew to open the gate. The bull sidesteps. Hooves catch air and land hard on packed dirt. Four, five, six. The space between Calvin and the bull widens. When he leans backward to reclaim his balance, the bull jerks left. In that instant Vandy sees his friend is too far right. Calvin flies out from the whirling brown and white, bounces once, and springs off one boot to clear the plunging bull. One hand clutches at the air where his hat was last. The bull stomps it flat and circles again, his horns aimed at Calvin's back. Calvin scrabbles up the fence. The fickle crowd roars.

"Close," Vandy says once his friend is up and outside. The bull trots back to his temporary pen.

Calvin mutters. "Yeah, that and a dollar will get you a stick-on tattoo, I Love Mom, in red ink."

At the crowd cheers, both men turn to watch the next pair, cowboy and bull in silhouette, up, down and sideways. "Seven, eight," the audience yells in unison.

"The Prince," Calvin sneers. "He sleeps with the bulls."

Vandy sucks back the laugh. Winning at this level is hard, but it's the same eight seconds as Nationals. And Joey Brudenheimer, aka the Prince, would as soon kick in your face as win. Although they don't use his nickname to his face, Brudenheimer has no friends. When luck is all you have and you may be the next up, being mean gets you nowhere. The Prince draws a small bull, on the verge of retirement and eager for pasture. Lucky draw. Without counting Vandy knows there are five more bulls. He knows them all. And he knows that Son of Crown of Thorns is still in line.

Glancing along the pens, he tries to figure out which contestants remain. While he recognizes the faces—most of them ride the circuit like he does—one or two new guys always show, gussied up in crisp jeans and full heels. Vandy only trusts cowboys with heels worn to the nails. If those guys drop a hint about a bull, you can believe them. Calvin's heels are so worn he rocks backwards when he stands in one place.

"Brother V, you see what I see?" Calvin says.

Vandy spins to look, his hat cocked back to let in the compressor-run lighting. He squints harder. "Who is that guy?"

The row of hats tilts up and follows the dust cloud of a kid, his big brother's chaps scrunched around his ankles. As if on ballerina toe shoes, he springs to the fence, hugs the rails, and struggles to fling one leg over. Once he's perched at the top, his gaze drills the bleacher crowd on the far side of the ring as if a signal there will tell him when to lower himself to the waiting bull. Vandy scans the stands too. When nothing catches his eye, he turns back to the kid.

Calvin moves up the fence to help him mount. Balanced, one leg cocked over the rail, he waits on the rider to settle in. "You sure you're ready for this, kid?" His words low, without judgment.

"Yeah, yeah," the boy answers, the necessary lie loud enough.

"Keep your back straight and your hips loose," Calvin offers.

"Right."

There is a long minute and a hush from the bleachers. Doubt hangs in the air. When the boy's hand shoots up, gate metal flashes silver in the generator lights. Cheers erupt. In the center of the ring the clown snaps his suspenders and reaches into his wide-waisted jeans. He draws out a cardboard cutout of a gun. With a wild wave, he points it at the plunging bull. A fake cannon explodes from the overhead speakers. The clown pretends to absorb the retort and falls. Dust buries him. The crowd roars. Calvin and Vandy are counting with the kid. The numbers on the digital timer flash. Four, five, six. Like a handkerchief a small white hand flutters above the bull's back. Seven, eight and the kid is in the air. He somersaults toward the fence, his face as blank and pale as a cadaver, his hat five feet higher.

"Damn," Calvin says. "The little shit's done that before."

"That's four made it."

It takes three guys to carry the kid out, his groans lost in the cheers. When the announcer calls the next name, an old black bull slurps into the cage. Con Man. They've all had him at least once. Sleepwalking, he dances right and then left and bows, same routine every time. Con Man is a guaranteed eight. Vandy holds his breath, but they don't call his name.

The other cowboy, grinning at his good fortune, climbs the rails two at a time and lowers himself onto the veteran's sway back. "Tough luck," the guy mouths the words to Vandy.

Vandy loosens the bandana at his throat. He'll be the last cowboy tonight, the encore. Through the rails he eyeballs the last bull, Son of Crown of Thorns, the meanest of the bunch and young enough to do some serious damage.

He should scratch. To hell with the seventy-five bucks. To hell with the long haul from Winchester. Any more broken ribs and he won't be able to drive the baler on Monday. If he loses that job, he'll never make the rent, much less Nationals. As he waits for Con Man to perform, he ekes out a silent prayer that the son of The Son has eaten a big dinner and lost interest in the game.

It takes the spectators a moment to realize that Con Man and the cowboy are loose because the bull eases out so slowly. It starts out like a pony ride, one hoof behind the other, no syncopation. The cowboy is confused. When his head tilts, Vandy wants to call out a warning, but it's too late. Just as he leans down, far enough to survey the bull's expression, the bull comes to, like a marionette whose strings snap taut. His back arches and all four hooves separate from the ground. Head raised, Con Man's horns slake the air in front of his rider. Although the rider pulls back, there's no time to correct his balance. Brown chaps and leather fringe and plaid shirt fly sideways and crumple against the fence post. The clown, jigging to the canned music overhead, reaches down and claws the cowboy off the ground just as Con Man, horns lowered, charges the red patch of shirt.

At the last second the bull swerves to avoid the metal rails and runs along the curved line of steel to the opposite end of the arena. By the time he makes it back to the open gate and his fodder reward, the cowboy has disappeared.

"Well, folks, just one more beggar in the final round tonight. Sodern," the announcer blasts through the microphone. "Vandy Sodern comes to us from all the way across the valley. Winchester. V. A. He's been trying for the Nationals three, four years now. Ain't that right, Vandy?" The announcer sweeps his ten-gallon off and replaces it in one smooth flourish. "He needs that paycheck tonight, folks, or he may be going home for good. Can he do it? Tell him what you think, fans. Give it up for Vandy Sodern."

Poised on the top, Vandy breathes deeply and ignores the burst of orchestrated cheers. On television they interview each rider before his event. They announce your hometown, your win-loss record, any unusual bull you've bested or vice versa. Nationals are the only place where they even pretend the cowboy is more important than the bull.

But here, in farming country, you ride your eight seconds mostly in the long shadows, the high intensity lights pointed into the atmosphere where they can't broadcast the stitching on your boots. Friends and strangers hold their breath, and you can't remember all the names of the girls who watch, girls you've slept with and girls who've slapped you away. There are no sponsors and your own money is on the line. Here the bull is king. It's important not to forget.

Metal whines across metal, the bull's feet thrum the ground. As hooves knock posts, the rails rattle back. Vandy reminds himself to stay focused. His own prayer is drowned by the spectators' shouts that rise up around him. He sinks onto the heaving back of Son of Crown of Thorns. The bull snorts, knocks the gate with the side of his head. Vandy grits his teeth. Eight seconds, he thinks, eight lousy marvelous seconds. And he raises his left hand to the stars.

The Genealogy of Secrets

Sarah Collins Honenberger

When little things began to disappear, Oma started to worry. One morning before church she missed her blue corduroy slippers. It wasn't long after she couldn't find the wooden pencil Ren had given her their first anniversary, made from a twig, the bark still on it. All spring she caught herself looking for something she'd seen the day before. The kitchen scissors, the sheep whistle, the birthday candles that couldn't be blown out. Everlasting they called them. Infuriating, Ren teased. None of the things was important. She could do without them. All together, though, their disappearance made an unsettling pattern. She couldn't shake the feeling that something bad was about to happen.

"Ren," she said at dinnertime one evening. An umber haze hung about the room in the warm dusk, the overbearing heat a surprise to her, though she ought to have adjusted to it after seven years here in this long, flat stretch of valley. They lived between two mountain ranges that hid West Virginia from the rest of the world. Despite sitting still, they were perspiring on the stiff oak chairs that were his mother's wedding present, a constant reminder that he'd been a son before he was a husband.

"Aya?" Ren didn't look up from the rhubarb pie. "Looket how this ice cream's melted into a river on the pie." His mustache dripped creamy white.

"Something's not right with Hilldrup," she finished.

"A cold agin?"

"I mean something lasting, that might never be right."

He plunged the spoon into the center of the pink and white, swirling it before he raised the spoon to his lips. "My mama tell you that?"

"Not exactly, but she acts funny around him." Oma felt a bit daring to speak critically of her mother-in-law, but the situation was too worrisome to hold inside any longer. Sometimes it felt as if his mother lived to catch them in a mistake. She'd as soon the entire county knew the most intimate details of their life than keep silent about even the tiniest fault of her only son's wife.

Oma had been raised in Tennessee on the wrong side of the Smoky Mountains. No one in Preston, West Virginia, considered her a fitting match for Rennick Hilldrup Forrester, especially not his mother. It didn't matter that Oma's great great-grandfather had been a candidate for senator from Tennessee or that her aunt had married into the Walker family of Johnny Walker fame or that Oma had been a steady and hard-working partner to Ren for seven years. She was not from West Virginia, and that was that.

While Ren waited for her to explain, he finished the pie. She loved that about him. He didn't interrupt. He didn't rant before he knew what was what. Oma scrambled to translate her vague feelings into details Ren could use to fix it. He loved to repair things.

Sometimes she lay awake in the middle of the night while he stretched out next to her—as quietly confident in his sleep as he was in the daytime—with his head buried in the feather pillow that Mother Forrester insisted was the only kind he should use. Hoping for a glimpse of the Milky Way, Oma would stare out the farmhouse windows and admit to herself that he'd married her because she'd needed fixing.

The night they met it had been raining for days. The trees were black with it. The bushes hung as heavy with it as if it had been shackles. Puddles ran into rivers by the curbs and into whirlpools by the drains. Her shoes, bought for dainty dance steps, flapped against the slick pavement, the cheap vinyl soles separated from the cardboard stiffeners. They'd been a gift from her boyfriend, Nick, who was forever bribing her with ridiculously useless presents.

She was on her way to the train station, fiercely determined finally to leave him and the wild jealousy that made him love her one minute and beat her the next. Her suitcase was barely a weight at all. She'd rescued her things from the rented room while he was in the bathroom tossing dinner and whiskey. As the rain and wind drove her along the empty street, the thrift store suitcase swung from her arm. Worried that he might follow her, she distracted herself by counting the day's tip money in her head, a comforting croon of lullaby to black out the ugliness of what she'd thought at the time was the final blow from Nick.

The station was silent and dark. After she walked around to the tracks, she put the suitcase down deep in the shadows. Gingerly, she touched her stomach. It still throbbed where he'd punched her, a physical reminder louder than the resolve in her heart that said she was better off out here in the storm.

Her back against the cold bricks, her dress soaked through, she closed her eyes. The train was due any minute. In the two months they'd been together she'd escaped mentally a dozen times, but always before had been hijacked by a sweetness that seeped from Nick the morning after, a tenderness no one else had shown her. For those few moments before he resumed the crass bravado that paralyzed her, he reminded her of her dead brother, Stith. And swept away by despair, she'd cling to Nick and the resolve to leave would vanish, a fleeting thought, impossible even to remember what or why.

Across the tracks, shapes shifted eerily in the night. Oma imagined other girls like herself, waiting and hiding. In the whole world there were no happy people—only those who hit and those who hid. Silently she prayed for those girls, without any grand gestures of chest heaving or fist pounding against breast. She prayed they would find the strength to climb the train steps and fly along the shiny rails to a new world. She imagined them sitting just so on the rough upholstery of the train seat, squeezed into a corner, glued to the window. She felt their terror over the possibility of a last-minute appearance by the man who had driven them to flee as clearly as if he'd bought the ticket personally.

In the empty night tires squealed and a door slammed. She told herself it was her imagination. But when Nick grabbed her arm, she screamed. He drew back, the sweetness long abandoned. But before his fist hit her jaw, one of the shapes leaped across the tracks and landed on his back. In the blackness she could only make out two massive hands on Nick's shoulders and then two figures were at her feet, rolling and clawing on the platform. For minutes, hours it seemed, they fought. The groans longer, the flailing less. When the train whistle blew, an arm from behind gathered her close and pushed her up the steps, the suitcase too. And the heavy metal door shut them off from the world.

The strange man sucked in the air in gasps, but he didn't look at her, his eyes on the receding tracks. "Sorry if I scared you."

She didn't know what to say. Afraid to concede any connection to Nick and wary of kindness, she wasn't ready to commit herself to a stranger, rescuer or otherwise. The last few months had taught her something.

When the man stepped away from the door and turned to face her, he didn't encroach, as if conceding her right to her own space. For all his height, his features were fine, like a child's. A ragged scar across his cheekbone left a smudged shadow in the gray light. She guessed he'd fought first on playgrounds. He didn't smile. And because he didn't, she knew he wasn't like Nick.

"Ren Forrester." His voice was slow and deliberate, the opposite of his piercing eyes. "You don't have to tell me your name," he said. "I'll call you Esmeralda." He picked up the suitcase. "How about coffee?"

Later, when she protested at his offer of a place to stay, he shuffled his feet and hesitated as if her going with him was as unimportant as the choice of who went through the doorway first.

"I live alone. My farm's two hundred acres and some. Paid for." It wasn't a boast, more like an introduction. "Sits on a hill, one road in so you can see who's coming ten minutes afore they get there. You can stay until you decide what you want." Perhaps he'd guessed already what she wanted.

Despite his prickly mother, they'd had a good seven years, better than she had a right to expect. And they had Hilldrup, thin still at seven and slow to fill out, but eager to please, affectionate, energetic.

But suddenly with something not quite right about him, that she was just beginning to notice now that he was in school. His eyesight was fine. The school nurse checked that first. Like a whiz he could put together puzzles and match dominoes. But he couldn't get along with the other children. With games, waiting for lunch, sharing markers, he bumped someone or knocked someone's chair and ended up in a fight. Yet he was never belligerent, always on the defensive. Still the bruises were a new constant. If this was how God and Mrs. Forrester had decided to punish her for the good years, she wished Ren had left her back at the train station. It wasn't fair to Hilldrup.

"Esmeralda?" Ren said, the old nickname calling her back from her musings. "You were telling about Hill." He stood up and, after he slid the plate into the soapy water, he put his arms around her and kissed her neck. "Don't go worrying over something you can't change."

"The teacher says he's not paying attention, but I know that's not right 'cause he works at it so. He tries so hard to follow the rules."

"Things are what they are, Oma. He'll be fine."

"They tease him."

"He never says a thing about it."

"They make fun of him."

"Not everyone's smart at book learning. He'll find something else."

She couldn't explain to Ren, the optimist, the practical fixer of things and people. Worry could make you fail, and the world's expectations could weigh you down until you didn't want to go on. She knew. She'd never told him about her family, about what her father had done, and about her brother. Some things were impossible to speak out loud.

Stith was part of the past, a past she'd put away during those early weeks on the farm, encouraged for the first time in her life to think of the future. Once Mrs. Forrester discovered her son had taken in a stray, it was too late to tell him about Stith. The longer it went without telling though, the more she felt she'd misled him.

He'd given her the front room with a view of the mountains. It turned out later to have been the parlor, but he never said. He just moved a bed from the storage shed into the room and jammed the sofa against the wall. He laid out fresh towels. Ignoring her pitiful suitcase, he found clothes for her. While he cooked, he showed her how to add the vegetables at the last minute to keep them crisp. In the evenings when the farm work was done, he read to her. The newspaper, his favorite childhood stories, even old letters from his grandparents. He brought her a quail egg and a snakeskin and an old bucket that he scraped and painted blue. She planted flowers in it and put it by the back door so he'd see it coming in after washing up.

That first fall, as they were getting to know each other, the rain came back. It flayed the trees and the ground as it had the night she'd left her old life. Terrorized by the drumming on the roof, she lay awake until she couldn't stand it any longer. She crept to Ren's room and crawled into his bed. They slept without touching and rose without speaking of it. At nightfall when he went up, still without a word from either of them, she followed. That was seven years ago.

Hilldrup called to her from upstairs, where he'd gone after dinner. She untangled herself from Ren. In the child's etched features, she saw her brother. The same transparent eyelids as Stith, the narrow chin, the pinched forehead burdened with worry lines. When Hilldrup looked up at her, she could be under the bridge again with Stith, hiding from the bullies. In Hilldrup's eyes she saw the same frustration.

Twice this year he'd been sent to the office for fights on the playground. The principal's note requested a conference in neat, typed lines addressed to both of them. She'd gone by herself, lied, and said Ren was away at a tractor convention.

Principal Hawkes lectured. Hilldrup needed to concentrate on schoolwork. He needed to stop picking fights. There was no getting in a word about the bullies. She wanted to ask about tutors or tests, but Principal Hawkes suggested a psychologist for anger control. She didn't know how she could manage that without Ren knowing. She didn't agree that Hilldrup was the one with the problem. That's when things started to disappear.

When she went up to say good night, Hill was lying on the bed.

"What's up, sweetie?" she asked.

Behind her, Ren's weight creaked on the stairs. She felt relieved not to have to deal with this by herself. Hilldrup mumbled into his pillow.

Ren spoke from over her shoulder. "Sit up, son, and tell us why you called your ma up here." Although she moved aside, Ren took her hand and held her there beside him. "We're all here together now. Let's hear it."

Oma felt the heat from Hill's gaze, more of a question than any words.

"Am I . . . did you . . . the kids say you found me in the hayfield, that you're not my parents."

She stood and went to the window so that he wouldn't see the tears. Ren didn't speak. They were both waiting for her.

"People make mistakes," she started. "They don't mean to hurt the people they love."

Hill put his hands over his ears. Ren yanked them away.

"Stop thet. You asked. If you're old enough to ask, you're old enough to hear the answer."

"Maybe we should . . ." She couldn't finish. What could she say now that would change what had happened back then? She'd been silent before and Stith had paid for that silence.

"I'll tell him," Ren said.

What would he tell when he didn't know the whole of it?

"Your mother was hurting when we met," he explained. "She couldn't talk about her life. Some things are too hard. You just don't talk about them. I loved her so I never asked. Later on when she married me, I figured she loved me too and whatever had happened before we were together didn't matter."

Oma kept herself still despite the desire to touch Ren, to feel the strength in his hands flow into hers. As if he sensed that wanting, he put his hand on the empty place on the bed where she'd been. But when she stayed at the window, he continued.

"You were born here in our house."

It sounded so simple. She wished she knew whether Ren believed it too or whether he had lived with her all this time, wondering. She could feel her son's eyes on her back, a demand for confirmation. She nodded her head, afraid to turn and risk disappointment from these two she loved more than anything in the world.

"But who is my real father?"

"He's dead." Although she spit out the word, it flooded her with memories.

"How did he die?" Hilldrup asked.

Stith's white face, twisted with shame for her, flashed in the darkened hallway again. The shouts and the shoving and the sharp burst from the gun all rushed at her. Gripping the edge of the dresser, she steadied herself. "There was an accident."

Ren came to her as if to shield her, as if Hilldrup were the dangerous one. "Oma," he said quietly.

"No, he needs to hear me say it," she whispered when she meant, *you need to hear me say it.* The words echoed back at her. Stith had loved her too, but it hadn't mattered. She stepped past Ren and put her back to the wall where she could see his face.

"I made a mistake," she said. "I didn't ask for help when I should have."

"Help for what?" In the boy's question she heard Ren's simplicity.

"My father drank too much."

Ren interrupted. "Your father?"

She continued, her voice edging higher. "He hit my mother. And then he'd come to my room, crying and feeling bad. I was afraid if I sent him away, he'd hit her again. I didn't tell anyone, not even my brother."

Ren's white face revealed all that he hadn't known.

"Stith stopped him," she whispered.

Ren's huge hands hung by his side, but his voice boomed. "That's enough."

She couldn't remember when he'd ordered her to do anything. Or not to. All this time she let him believe it was Nick. But Nick hadn't been the beginning. He'd been her solution to the guilt. It was easier.

Sinking onto the bed, Ren moved his hand gently over the boy where he lay motionless, his eyes wide. As she watched, she saw the truth for what it was, a wall, a fist, to drive them apart. Some truths were worse than lies. If she'd told Ren sooner, the choice could have been his. She owed him an apology, but it was too late.

He scooped Hilldrup into his arms. "We're going down to the porch to look at the stars."

Alone, she lay down on the bed and breathed in the smell of her son. It surrounded her: fresh shampoo, perspiration damp on his pillow. All around her, his little boy things. He'd hardly lived long enough to collect much, yet the room was full. On the bulletin board hung a picture of the three of them fishing from the dinghy. Her mother-in-law had photographed them from the dock. The bookcases overflowed with books and odd bottles, a dented pair of binoculars from the church bazaar, and his softball mitt. And there, stuck between the books, she saw the missing candles, still in their box, and, on the bottom shelf, her corduroy slippers. A child's collection of talismans to prove he belonged.

Moonlight had filled the room by the time Ren came back with a sleeping Hilldrup. Awake instantly, she rose and straightened the sheets so Ren could lay him down. She struggled to tell him she would rent a room in town, she wouldn't burden him any longer, but the words filled her throat and she couldn't speak. After covering the boy, she touched the back of her fingers to his cheek, flushed, smooth. Ren put his hand over hers, there on Hilldrup's forehead, the connection so strong the words of regret fell away and she couldn't breathe at the wonder of it.

"Stay," he said.

It was the first time he had asked and she knew, at last, that she could.

What You Need to Know About the Mountain

Erin Newton Wells

(First place fiction, *Skyline* contest, 2017)

"You know she's not right in the head," says Lurlene.

I stir my coffee, freshly brewed the way my grandmother did, the Queen Mum, rest her lovely soul.

"Pthew. What the heck is that?"

She picks a fleck from her tongue and examines it.

"Eggshell," I say, without looking.

You would think she might remember it by now. With Lurlene, the board wipes clean every day. How many mornings does she sit here at my table and gripe about the coffee? How many times does she return? She drags the offending bit off her thumb onto the edge of the saucer, making a show afterward of wiping her hands on her shirt.

"I want egg," she mutters, "I ask for omelet."

I smile sweetly, true to my upbringing. The shells are always washed, of course. They help settle the grounds, or so the lore would have it. I am not going into it today.

"Sal-mo-nel-la," she enunciates.

"Maybe I'll go into town after awhile," I say, packing her obsession and driving it right down the road, no return trip.

She will expand this to botulism, then *E. coli*. We will have a lecture on the sanitary practice of handling food. If you do not head it off at the pass, we visit ebola and, what is that new one, the latest mosquito thing.

"Oh, I could do that," says Lurlene. "I've got the morning free. I could pick up my vitamin powder at the drug store. And pomegranate juice. Antioxidant. You have to keep the level up."

She slides with accustomed ease into the passenger seat, already talking her way into town.

"Or maybe," I close that door, "I shall weed around the shed while it still feels cool."

"You got a groundhog out there. Big fat son of a gun."

"Really?"

"Dug itself a hole wide as God back of that shed. Turn your ankle in it."

"Think of that."

By which I mean, help yourself, dear heart. Go right ahead. Tour the property any old time. My shed is your shed, which pretty much is the way Lurlene sees it.

"They'll destroy a foundation quick as greased monkeys. Big fat rats is what I call them. They multiply, tunnel under a place. You need to roust it out, hit it on the head with a shovel. That would fix its clock."

"I dare say. Well." I take a sip. Monkeys, rats, God, clocks. She is in fine fettle today.

Sleek and spice brown, his sides ripple as he scurries through the clover. I call him Ralph, after my ex. But at least we are off the trail of deathly diseases and probiotics. The window at the table is open to the sun. It gives the perfect view of my patch of ground, including the shed, imperiled as it is. No sign of Ralph yet. Lurlene probably spooked him back to bed. He reclines in comfort in the palatial burrow, the extent of which as yet undetermined.

Good old Ralph. The ex, not the groundhog. He is quite lean, not plump like the marmot that bears his name. But he scuttles here and there, sampling this and that, cannot sit still, cannot stick to one spot for long. Nibble, nibble, nibble, goes Ralph across the yard, the town, all the way across the state line to yet another fantastic job.

You will not believe how great this opportunity is. He announces the next one in a string of many. Ralph's new toy, which, of course, does not last long. It soon breaks or wears out, like all the rest. It comes to this. I cannot follow him anymore. I cannot do it. I like to put down roots, and they need to be in this particular patch of good soil.

"Maybe someone dropped her on her head when she was a baby," says Lurlene.

She shoves her cup away, unfinished, making sure I notice.

"What? Oh."

True to form, she makes a U-turn and comes back to Posey.

"She's just old, Lurlene. Don't be unkind."

"Been loony ever since I knew her. Fifteen years? When did I move to my place? Fifteen sounds right. And you've been here a coon's age. Or your family has."

Add coons to the list, a growing menagerie. Subtract from the coon's years the few I followed after Ralph. The ex, not the marmot.

"Posey is a free spirit," I say.

"Her kids should have hauled her out and put her somewhere safe."

"You think they haven't tried?"

"Pick up the chair she's in. Carry it out of the house. Done deal."

Clock fixed.

"It certainly is one approach."

Good old Posey, the village wacko. Just wait until your turn, my friend. But the friend does have a point. Posey has taken a turn, a little more dotty these days and given to wandering in her nightgown outside. She stands in the yard and sings. But Posey always sings, ever since I met her.

These are my morning songs, she tells me. My midday songs. My night songs. Songs for the calling of cats. Songs for the breaking of bread. Songs for the planting of cucumber.

And why not, I ask you?

Beyond the shed is the fence the Great Gilhooley made, or GGH for short, along with the Queen Mum, or QM, which will be the grandparents. They built the place with considerable grit, as the story goes. He wins the land on a wager, the GGH does, with his sweet Irish gift of gab.

G-hooley Junior maintains it, which will be my dad, along with my mum. Now it is mine. After all the effort and history, can I leave this hallowed ground? No, thank you, sir. I tried. It did not work.

Ralph never sees it this way. His family moves a thousand times, restless for new space. Here, there, nibble, nibble. To each his own. I wish him well. But I am made of this rich, lovely dirt.

42

Beyond it, Boggy Noggin rears its endearing and oddly shaped head. It somewhat resembles an egg, but a densely forested green one, especially now in summer. The QM names it, although no true bogs will be found there, only cool grottoes in which to imagine yourself a toad princess or the finder of the secret door under the mountain.

I think of it as peaceful now. But as a child, Noggin could scare me deliciously. Anything could live in those shadows, those holes among the roots. And at night? Well.

"So what do you think?" Lurlene leans forward.

"Mmm?"

Her arm lies across the table, the inner side exposed, fingers extended, palm up. A couple of small bites dot it. She points them out. Otherwise I might not notice.

"Lyme or Zika? Something bit me good yesterday. I'm not seeing the bull's-eye yet, so I'm guessing Zika. You know if anyone here went to South America, like Brazil? Or Puerto Rico? Or Florida?"

No one here travels much past the post office or the Piggly Wiggly, except Ralph. The ex. I stare at the red spots, then her.

"Beats me."

"I should report it. I'm not feeling all that well. Maybe a fever."

I study her broad face, freckles across the nose, sun-battered hair. Lurlene, the pastoral picture of health.

"Give it until tomorrow, at least. I have a tube of hydrocortisone. Do you want it?"

"With all that stuff they put in? Petrochemicals? No way, girly. That's an outright invitation to cancer, and I'm not singing that song."

* * * *

Songs for the going out and coming in, Posey tells me. For the celebration of the damselfly that hovereth on the water. Hovereth. She says this.

Posey, with the long white braid down her back, moving like a rustic Isadora Duncan in her rambling yard

43

among the vines of cucumber and the halos of dill on their tall stalks, the trellis of Concord grapes full of wasps. They never sting her. She swishes them aside with her hand.

"They mean no harm," she says. "They just do what wasps are put here to do. They like grapes as much as the rest of us. Who am I to tell them no?"

Posey, sharing the earth and the fruits of her labor. She used to wear that braid wrapped around her head in a crown. Lately she lets it fall, unpinned. Everything goes easier and looser, a soft gown to wear instead of changing into something else.

The cats insinuate themselves between us and lounge in the shade. They perch on the porch rail, swinging their tails in syncopated songs of their own.

"You know, Peggy," she tells me one day when I stop by. She pulls me aside and turns my shoulders so I face the Noggin. "How many chances do you get to see such a thing? Can you count how many never get to see it? Can you? Take a good look. Look and look and look until it settles inside."

She heaves out a breath, her thin robe flapping in a bit of air. The knobby knees show, then hide, and her bare toes curl into the dirt.

"You have to let some things go," she says.

Posey, my druid, the GGH would say, were he here to observe. So I think it for him, a druid in the garden among the dill, the air full of spirits.

One night he calls me to him and says, "Pegeen."

At the time, I shrink from the name he always uses, my birth name. The old-country sound of it embarrasses me when I am young.

"Pegeen. I plan to walk up that mountain tonight. And will you go with me?"

What do you say to such an absurd question? You say, "Yes, Great One." I am eight. The thrill of it courses through my blood. My breath jams in my lungs. I am chosen.

"At night," he says, "we see things we cannot see in the day. It is practical to know both, so as to be prepared."

I do not ask, prepared for what? I still have hopes of the creatures the QM talks about, having seen them once in her youth. She chooses a comfortable evening, prepares me for sleep, and tells me her tales of the dreams that come out from under the mountain.

That night I follow behind him, as he tells me to. I step where he first steps to test the ground. We climb through the forest, the mountain growing enormous. Every sound, every slight whisper, turns me cold until it becomes hilarious, and I laugh. I cannot help myself. Then I cry.

He sits me down on the forest floor, on the dark, cool needles of pine.

"Get a grip, lass," he says. "Pegeen, Pegeen. It is only old Noggin without his colors."

No. This place has no name. But I do not say this to him.

"Just some ways farther. Then you'll see."

So we go on until the top, the egg, which is more bald than not. He does not need to point out what he wants me to find. The full moon floods the open space, my face turned up to it, everything bathed and changed. I can put my hands on the disk of it. I can put my mouth to it and eat and swallow until I am full of the silver-white light.

I do not know that in half a year he will be gone. I am too young to see the signs. It is as much for him as for me. Hold on. This is what we climb for and reach.

* * * *

"So let's say I call him. That righteous, holy nurse picks up and says I should watch it. I should call back in a few days if I don't see any improvement. And I think, hello. I am calling you because I don't see any improvement. Can you hear, or would you like me to say it louder? A few days and I could be dead and dandy. Is that what you want? She'd never even let me talk to the great doctor."

I focus on her talking mouth, her cup still full, mine half gone, the QM's coffeepot parked on the stove and making its warm, burbling sounds. Irish, but she preferred coffee to tea, said it was that odd strain of German in her. Those invaders, she laughed.

"So, do they want me to roll up and die of this? Would that convince them?"

She thrusts her arm at me and waves it like a flag, the small stars of bites swooshing back and forth.

"I wouldn't think so. No." I search. "Maybe put some ice on it. Elevate it. That could always help."

Or count to one hundred. Make a wish. Say three Hail Marys. Recite the Gettysburg Address. Run widdershins around the house, then run back the other way to cancel bad luck. That should do it, or fix its clock.

"Just you wait. The whole place comes down with Zika. Hey there, folks. Did I try to warn you? And did you listen? And is there any vaccine yet? Is there?"

Lurlene eyes me, rises, and puts her cup and saucer in the sink. She exits with a flair, the tier of temple bells chuckling at the door.

I see her cross the yard and let herself through the gate. It whines in its need for oil. Ralph waits a beat or two and emerges beside the shed, which he has undermined, no doubt, with abandon. He stands straight up, as marmots do, sniffing the disturbed air before he drops to the grass and continues his breakfast.

I give her time to clear, then walk down the road to check on Posey and see if she needs anything. She is not outside. The door is never locked. I go in. I call. Nothing. No Posey.

Her sad house is a shell slowly returning to whatever it was, the elements out of which it grew, crumbling mildly, considering each day another thing to let go. Dishes are unwashed, and clothes are scattered. The cats mill and nap, but no sign of her. It feels hollow.

Songs for going out. Songs for the slow times of the heart and the memory of days. I am listening and searching. Let me find her first. Let me not have to call with the news.

"Posey is not right in the head," says Lurlene.

And who would be, as vines send their networks through the mind, shadowing with their interlace of leaves and covering all the things we know. The damselfly hovereth over water. She still knows this. My name, sometimes. The names of

46

the cats, some of them. Her name. The words for cucumber and grape, mostly. We all have our days.

She remembers how to sing. This is an old, old part of us, going back to that loose, formless time when we listen to the voices of our mothers and are rocked by them. She remembers songs, or bits of songs, the best bits.

She remembers old places. How many chances do you get to see such a thing? Look and look and look until it settles inside. Of course. I should know. Look and look. I should know to start there.

* * * *

By afternoon I find her, halfway up Noggin on the trail and hidden by the trees. She sits cradled in the great roots, her knees pulled up, and she weeps. I have never seen Posey cry.

"I don't know," she says. "I don't know where I am."

I sit beside her, put my arms around her, hold her tightly. I lean her head against me and smooth the brow, the long white hair loose from its braid, an accidental wreath of leaves and twigs tangled in it. I rock her.

"I don't know," she weeps.

"Were you always called Posey?" I ask. "Is Posey short for something else?"

"Rosemary. For remembrance."

There. Sharp and fast as can be.

"Rosemary. A lovely plant, a lovely fragrance," I say.

"I don't know."

"Ring around the rosie," I begin.

"Pocket full of posies," she sings.

"Good old Noggin." Everyone here calls it this, after the QM christens it.

"Noggin," she says, calming.

"Why wouldn't you go here, Posey, given the chance? Can you count how many never get to see such a thing? You were wise to do it while you can."

She shakes her head, stretches her legs, flexes her toes.

"So many going in and out, they never see," she says. "Right here before them."

47

"Right here. And they never see. Let me tell you how the moon looks at night from up there." I point to the trail. "The top, like an egg."

"Like an egg," she nods. "I know." So many times she goes there.

"You reach up and take the moon and put it in your mouth and eat. And all inside, you are light," I say. "You let it settle into you."

She laughs, nodding, "Yes. Yes."

"You can carry it with you."

"Yes," she says, pounding her fists on her thin legs. Leaves flutter from her hair into the lap of her summer gown.

The GGH nods. I touch my forehead in salute.

* * * *

That night I tuck her into bed in the spare room and put a night light for her. Tomorrow I will call her son and daughter. I will see to the cats. I will water the cucumber and dill and the trellis of grapes.

I ask her to sing me a song before going to sleep, and she sings one for the night, about how the trees close in, their branches over her, how the moon catches in them. She puts it in her mouth, a sweet lozenge, and thinks of nothing but that. Whatever comes out from under the mountain does not trouble her.

"Good night, Posey," I tell her, stooping to kiss her smooth cheek. The skin is cool. Her face is calm. I have brushed her hair into a cloud.

"Goodnight," she says. "I do not know who you are. But I love you."

If a Tree Falls

Erin Newton Wells

(First place fiction, Blue Ridge Writers Contest, VWC, 2017)

"You having a fit?"

Two bare feet plant themselves beside me, the toenails painted plum with specks of glitter in the polish. The feet divide a lush emerald grass. In my hands the last clots of grass fall and stick to everything. Around us the black dirt smells of water. I am crazy with extravagance.

This is how the map begins in the crescent of the east. It moves into a swath of yellow-green, then yellow, the colors heating as they move west. It crosses the spine of the continent to flat brown, dead orange, smoldering vermilion. I should take the hint.

But I am busy with myself, following best offers, gathering honors and credentials. A few years here, a few years there, until where I am becomes too hot to touch.

At midday I do not go out. Sun pounds the ground and dares it. Whatever grows has a bitter hull to contain the spirit inside. I cannot live like this. I cannot live with one who does, although at first he seems charming.

"No hard feelings," he says.

"Right. Okay," I agree. Paper pods clatter on mesquite trees, tumbleweed at the door, rattlers in dry arroyos.

"Sometimes things just don't turn out." He gives the door of the car a thump in a show of good will. He even checks the pressure of the tires before they begin to roll on the boiling asphalt.

I cannot think of another thing to say.

Sometimes things go dormant in the desert, where it almost never rains. Sometimes the prince is a lizard after all and you never know, not easy to spot at first. It beguiles with its bright black eyes. You think it harmless. You get used to how it controls you.

I am wedged among cartons and bags of my minimized life with the air squeezed out.

Good-bye, we wave through dust and sun, his figure a slithering mirage in the heat of the road. I am done with it and portable again, ready to return to the cradle of civilization.

One day out, and the air conditioner fails. I drive by night with windows open and leave the blazing state behind. I miss nothing of it, not spines or thorns, not reptiles or poisoned toads.

Five days out, and the air turns merciful. I drive by day with pillars of cloud before me, a wealth of cooling moisture. In the rear view, I catch myself as a wasp on fire, still burned by the desert, still trying to survive. I hunch forward. Intensely black glasses wrap my face. Red hair explodes from the wad screwed and pinned to my head.

The engine goes silent on the road shoulder, and silence becomes a dizzy fly and one distant bark. Grass covers the fields. Kudzu creeps. It climbs a line of trees and changes them.

The green soothes with its pillowed shapes. I want to lie on them and sleep. They squander themselves, with or without me.

"Lizard," I say, climbing out and stretching full length.

I feel the grass pliable and soft. Light does not threaten and slam. It measures itself with shadow. The land is full of grace.

"Lizard!"

Now to the rolling, kicking, flinging.

I rip handfuls of this living stuff and waste it, bunch after bunch, over my head, my fingers stained green.

"You have a fit?"

Bare feet, toenails painted plum.

Here we are.

"I don't have a spoon on me. Stick might do. Stepbrother get a fit like this. Bite his tongue off. Leprosy."

I brush grass from my face.

"So, lady, you have a fit?"

"I'm okay."

I sit up.

"Well, you got something. Don't take much to see it."

"Not leprosy."

50

She's maybe fourteen, skinny, but starting to look womanish in Daisy Mae shorts and midriff top. Her lips are the same plum, the eyes coated turquoise, black hair short and spiky, like she cuts it herself and dyes it with ink.

"So how come you wallowing out here? Nothing but a fool does that."

She squats beside me

"It's been a long time since I saw real grass and trees," I say.

"You blind or something?"

"They don't have it where I come from."

"No such place, or I'm a pop-eyed booger."

She stares hard at the black shields that cover my eyes.

"Why'd you come back if you was someplace else? Me, I'm headed to California."

"Walking?"

"Dumb. See this?"

She waggles a thumb in my face.

"Hook the first sucker come along. You're aimed the wrong way."

"Why?"

"Like, really? Who'd stay in this dump?"

"Didn't anyone tell you creeps prowl the roads? You're lucky it was me."

"They don't scare me none."

Just fields. No houses in sight. Still a few miles from town.

"Where do you live?"

Shrug.

"Let me give you a ride back to your house."

"Don't have one."

"Sure you do."

"Tanya kicked me out, said go feed your own mouth, got too many brats. Who needs her anyway. So I cut out. Same's Mama."

"She left, too?"

"She's a whore. Mamaw run her off, says go somewhere I never see you. Mamaw died from cigarettes. Coughed up her dumb lungs."

51

My hair comes loose.

"Good color," the girl says. "I'd do mine like that. Should bleach first. Which one you use?"

"What?"

"Color. You stupid?"

"Look, how old are you?"

"Eighteen."

I stare her down.

"Fifteen." Shrug.

"I'll give you a ride to town. There's places you can stay overnight."

"Dumbsville? Those goody-goody joints? Give you a plate of slop and stick a Bible in your face. No way."

She brightens. "I can stay with you."

"My place is tiny. I've got lots of work to do."

"What kind a work? I can work."

"I'm going back to school. Dumbsville made the best offer."

She snorts. Slaps her hand against the ground. Snorts again.

"You're too old for school."

"Thanks. I'm thirty. I'm guessing your school starts soon."

"I plan to be a beautician. Don't need booger school."

"Yeah? I hear they have to go to school, too."

Pursed lips. Narrowed eyes. The fume.

"By the way, I'm Jack."

"That's stupid. Why you got a boy's name?"

"Family secret. What's yours?"

She thinks about it.

"Lutie. But I'm changing it to Luticia."

In the end I convince her by offering to spring for pizza.

Kudzu drapes the sides of the railroad bridge. Giant oaks shade the street. The university relaxes into its mannered lawn. We find a place across from it, and Lutie falls into her food. For the price of a meal I get more of the sketchy story. Anyone can see why Lutie chooses the roadside instead.

She's grabbing bread sticks from other tables when I return from making phone calls.

"They have room. I'll take you there."

Her shoulders stiffen.

"That homeless dump? You think I'm that dumb?"

"You can't stay on the street. It's with other women."

"They'd send me right back."

"Not if it's not safe."

"What do you know about anything? You eat that piece?"

I hand it over.

"I can cook. I do good mac and cheese. I can fix up your place."

I shake my head.

"They can get you into a jobs program."

"Not doing none a that."

"Lutie, I can't afford it. I've got no legal rights."

"I can get my own job. I can do nails."

"Don't you understand? I've got no legal rights. I can't just take you in."

She slides lower in the chair.

"I'm good at nails."

"No deal."

The fume.

She manages to fit in the front seat of the car by holding boxes on her lap. The shelter is not too far and on the way to my apartment. I make the mistake of pointing it out as we pass. Stupid. Repeat after me.

"So I drop dead. Who cares." arms crossed.

She refuses to look as I leave her at the check-in desk.

"Nobody gives a booger I live or die."

"Wrong," I say.

The attendant gives me a tired smile, but Lutie will not look at me.

The building is dwarfed by one enormous oak and a cluster of locust trees. Flowering hedges crowd the porch. I could walk to my place from here if I needed to.

* * * *

53

Mailed book cartons wait in front of the door. I shove them inside. Next day I go on campus to stake out a cubbyhole and talk to my adviser. I meet a couple of other TAs.

By the time I walk home, I'm ready to hit the sack. I nearly stumble over her on the step.

"Lutie! What are you doing here?"

"Gnawing my dumb arm off I'm so hungry."

"The shelter feeds you."

"Stinks. Like I said. I can't eat that slop."

"Oh, Lutie." I sink beside her.

"Stomach's caved in. About to die."

"I can't do pizza tonight. I'm really tired. I've already explained."

"Anything'll do. Piece a bread."

The turquoise eyes are wearing off, and the plum lips. She's starting to look more like a child with a bad haircut.

"Come on." I let her in. "But then it's back to the shelter."

Lutie spends the night on a pallet in the tiny apartment.

In the morning, breakfast is ready with bread and peanut butter cut in triangles and arranged on a plate, like the night before. The pallet is neatly rolled. Book cartons are moved from the entrance and lined under a window near the shelves.

"I could unload all that," she says.

"I've got to go to work. I'll walk you to the shelter. That's it."

The attendant takes the absence in stride. She slips me the information. There's no family in the area with a Tanya, no boy with epilepsy, no mother of ill fame, no grandmother that died of cigarettes, so far as they can tell. Lutie carries no identification. Maybe she's a floater from somewhere else.

The director is checking into emergency foster care, but it takes time.

Lutie looks out the window, her arms and chin pressed on the sill. The oak pushes large leafy branches against the glass. The light coming in makes her arms pale green.

That evening she waits on the steps. Her eyes are turquoise again. She wears dangling earrings in the shape of crescent moons. I ask if she bought them.

"Somebody give them to me."

The pattern continues. I go to school. Lutie pretends to go to the shelter. In the evening she's on the step, with additions to her scant belongings.

The plum lips reappear, then a gauzy pink shirt over a tank top, then rhinestone flip-flops. A small purse on a long strap looks expensive, a buttery soft leather. The tag says España. She claims she found it empty on the sidewalk, no way to return it.

After a meager meal, Lutie sits on the floor with two bottles of nail polish. She applies a fresh coat of glittered plum to her toes, then paints tiny dots of cerulean. I'm running out of food. I'm trying to concentrate on a journal I need to read. But my eyes keep straying.

"Did you find the polish, too?"

"I found this nail place. They had my color!"

"So you bought it?"

"They give it to me. Since I like it so much."

I return to my journal.

"They said maybe I could get a job there." She paints blue dots. "You got kids?"

"No."

"And you're already that old? I had a kid."

"What?" I look up.

"Last year. Dead-born. Tanya says, good, don't need no more brats."

I lose my place in the article.

Lutie paints her toes. "What'd you do where you use to live?"

"Teach." My voice sounds squeezed.

"Why in boogerland you need to go to school if you was a teacher?"

I say it gently. "So I can learn how to teach teachers."

"So you hate what you did where you was?"

"No, I liked it."

"But you cut out. You got fired?"

55

"No."

"That's dumb. Somebody throw you out? Beat up on you?"

"Sometimes things just don't work out."

"Hanh." She finishes the dots.

* * * *

On Thursday, I develop a sick headache and go home to lie down at my lunch break. Lutie lounges on the floor, ear buds in, iPod in hand. She doesn't hear the door and jumps when I step beside her. She yanks out the buds.

"The big rule, Lutie," I say, slowly framing words in steel-edged units. "You are not here when I am not here. Got it?"

She hunches into her shoulders, sticks out a plum lip. A new crystal heart glimmers at her neck.

"I locked the door. How did you get in?"

She nods at the window above the book cartons.

"It was locked. I lock everything. I check the locks. You broke in."

The lip. The shrug.

"I was fixing that for you."

On the sill a paper cup from a fast-food place holds a length of kudzu vine. A string runs around the window frame. The vine coils onto it.

"You like green stuff." She looks sideways at me. "Rolled in it like a pig when you come from that place didn't have none. Grows faster'n spit. Week or two you look out, all you see is dumb green stuff."

It's the first time I hear her laugh.

"Thank you." My neck throbs at the back of my skull.

"You don't look so hot, Jack."

It's the first time she calls me by name.

"Heavy duty headache," I say.

"I'm good at this." She begins kneading the tight shoulders. "I could be a massager."

"You could." The tightness eases.

56

"It's great, Lutie. Really. But it doesn't get you off the hook."

I cannot hold my tongue.

She removes her hands like I burned them.

"And I'd like to know about the iPod. Are you going to tell me someone gave it to you?"

She tightens her lip.

"I have to be able to trust you, and the stories are getting thin."

"I'm telling the truth!" She snatches the purse. "You're the one I can't trust! I can't trust nobody! Nobody cares I live or die!"

The turquoise eyes shoot sparks.

"Keep your booger trust. Your booger books. Your booger," she turns around, looking, "booger everything!"

The door slams behind her. The window rattles. The kudzu shakes in its disposable cup.

I limp to an afternoon class and try to get through the rest of the day with lightning bolts in my head.

She doesn't appear at night. The shelter hasn't seen her. I need groceries but stay at the apartment, just in case. The kudzu visibly grows.

On Friday morning, I need to be on campus. I'm tempted to leave the window unlocked, but rules are rules.

I detour by the shelter.

"Don't take it personal," the attendant says. "These kids float. Nothing to hold them. Our hands are tied."

"You think she's still around here someplace?"

"A million and one places. But you're not likely to find them. They hide in plain sight, slip through cracks like smoke."

"Or hitchhike out?"

"Might have."

Or things we don't want to imagine.

"Guess it's your first time to step in this." She gives the smile. "I seen it too many times. Never easy."

Stay safe, Lutie. Stay away from sly things.

At the market I stop for fruit, bread, peanut butter. Lutie cleaned me out. I watch the sidewalk for bare feet, flip-flops, painted toes, too many in a college town. All these new ones cross the multicolored map to end up here. Those already here cannot wait to get out. The ones born to this green think they suffocate and head for the molten sun or do not think at all and just go. Such coming and going, noticed or not, rising or falling.

I walk home under the railroad bridge where kudzu climbs the embankment. I pass under the oaks that began in colonial times. All this greenness grows in silence.

No one is on the step. I open the door to find the vine grown another inch. It creeps each day until it covers the window. It will fill the room and make no sound.

Finding Canaan

Deborah M. Prum

(Second place fiction, *Skyline* contest, 2017)

Hanover, New Hampshire

I slouched in the backseat, hung over from a night of partying. Jane hunched behind the steering wheel of her yellow Dodge Colt hatchback, grinding the gears as she shifted from first into second. Andi read a map, intermittently shouting directions. My tongue felt furry. A dull ache throbbed through the meninges of my brain.

Jane's chipper voice did not help. "Tia, you're gonna love the leaves. They don't have color like this in San Francisco." My housemate, Jane, had insisted we three go on the hike and also had appointed herself as the tour guide.

I barely looked up. Each ray of the morning sun felt like a sharp knife stabbing directly into my head.

Andi, who hailed from Texas, said, "These colors are gorgeous." Then she lowered her glittery sunglasses and said, "Tia, darling, you're a little grumpy. Too many margaritas last night?"

Hanover is a sleepy college town in the middle of nowhere. What else is there to do but get wasted on a Friday night?

One could smoke dope. Marijuana certainly takes the edge off for me. I'll admit I am wired. Most days, I'm still bouncing off the walls at midnight, my thoughts jittery, batting against the sides of my skull. Is dark energy causing the universe to expand at an accelerating rate? Will my mother remember to send the rent check? I usually slip into a fitful sleep around two. But by five, I'm wide awake again, my brain speeding in circles, squares, and big elliptical loops. Yesterday, I'd agreed to a hike up Carlton Mountain, forgetting that an early Saturday morning comes directly after a late Friday night.

"Wait, wait! Is this Canaan?" Andi slipped off her sunglasses to get a better look at the map. "Did we just pass Route 118?"

Jane hit the brakes and then jerked the steering wheel to the right. My stomach lurched. After locating the trailhead sign, we pulled into a parking area. I staggered out of the car, dry-popped two aspirin, and rested my head on a splintery picnic table.

Jane unfolded the trail map. "Okay. We can manage this one. The West Ridge Trail. Only a mile-and-a-half up."

I lifted my head. "We'll have to take rest stops."

"Oh, you're gonna love this hike. Says here that a fire in the 1850s burned all the trees at the top. So it's open rock. Good views of Newfoundlake. Plus, there's a lookout tower we can climb." Jane studied the map. "We can return on the logging road that starts at the tower. It's flat and wide. Only four miles. We'll end up a little north of the parking lot."

"Four miles?" I wanted to cry. "Can't stay out that long. I've got about a thousand pages to read before Monday morning."

"You already were a physics major, then you added philosophy. What were you thinking?" Andi patted my head. Even her slight touch hurt.

Jane took three tries to fold the map. "Eighteen credits plus that EMT course. You're crazy."

"Advanced first aid, not EMT."

Leaning heavily on the picnic table, I stood and said, "All right. Time to begin our bonding experience."

As we climbed, the sky darkened and the air temperature dropped. I wished I'd brought a heavier jacket or at least a hat. I felt as if I had twenty pounds of lead in each leg. Andi wore cowboy boots and seemed to be struggling too. Jane scurried ahead.

At one point I steadied myself against a tree. Andi stopped too. "Tia, honey, you look puny."

"Head's pounding. The cold just exacerbates it."

Andi sat down. She opened up her massive backpack, considering this was supposed to be a three-hour hike. "Here," she said, "You can un-exacerbate the cold with this."

She gave me a knit hat. Pink. I detest pink. But it would provide warmth. I jammed my hair into the hat.

Andi glanced back. "You look striking in pink."

Prepared for any clothing contingency, Andi pulled a powder-blue canvas hat from her pack, the kind Dobie Gillis used to wear on *Gilligan's Island*. She arranged it over her big blond hair. "Your head wouldn't hurt so much if you drank less. Why do you go to those horrible parties?"

Jane turned. "Be nice, Andi."

"Yes, be nice, Andi. I'll share a secret with you. I'm searching for the perfect guy."

"At a frat party? Right. The both of you'd be too plastered to know you've found true love." Andi frowned.

"Not everybody is inebriated all of the time."

Jane actually stopped scurrying for a minute to say, "Inebriation is one issue, but I think perfection is the bigger issue. Tia, there aren't any perfect guys. You aren't perfect. How can you demand perfection?"

"I just want a different life from what my parents had."

"What do you mean?" Jane looked puzzled.

"It would take hours to fill you in." Even though we had known each other for a year, I had been vague about my family.

"We got nothing but time. And I adore a good story." Andi loved to know the gruesome details about everybody's family. She loved even more to tell you about hers. Once Andi gets going, her speech is pure stream of consciousness, with no tangent too obscure to explore. In addition, the more deviant the family member, the more detail you have to endure.

I decided to stick to the bare-bones facts of my family history. "My mother, Brita, met my father, Carlo, at an embassy party in Rome. She left the event with Carlo that night. She never bothered to go back to her own husband and two teenage sons in Stockholm." I didn't like to talk about this aspect of my mother.

"She abandoned her kids?" Jane sounded appalled.

"They were older, not babies." As if I really believed that excused my mother's behavior.

Andi asked, "What did Carlo look like? Some kind of Roman god?"

"Not exactly. He was a compact man. Probably gray hair by that time."

Andi laughed. "A tiny Roman god."

"I can't say what the attraction was. He moved her to a luxurious house on Nob Hill in San Francisco. That's a mystery too, since the offices for his shipping company were in Livorno, Italy, and New York City."

"Did they get married right away?" Andi loved weddings. She planned imaginary ones all the time.

"I don't know if they ever got married. Never have seen any evidence of it. For all I know, Carlo may have had another family in New York or Italy. I arrived exactly nine months after they met."

"So he didn't live with you in California?"

"Oh, he breezed through every few months or so. They talked on the phone every couple of days. He took care of us in grand style. We had a housekeeper and when I was little, a nanny. Carlo paid big bucks for me to go to school at the Convent of the Sacred Heart. Mom always drove a new-model Mercedes."

"Were you close to him?"

"I never even called him Dad, just Carlo. The man referred to me as 'the girl' as in 'How is the girl doing?' With his accent, it came out, the 'girlah.'"

"Did your mother tell you about the embassy party?"

"Oh no. She kept tight-lipped about her past life. When I was about ten, I discovered her diary. I have half-brothers named Ulf and Johan. As far as I know, none of them has ever been in contact since she left. I've never bothered to look them up."

We walked silently for a few minutes. "Carlo died in Singapore of a heart attack when I was seventeen. Carlo's lawyer informed my poor mother by telegram several days after the fact. Carlo left her plenty of money but didn't mention me in his will. The rat. About three months later, my mother married Henry, her tennis partner from the club. They'd eaten lunch together on Thursdays for years."

"Do you like him?" Jane always wished her widowed father would remarry.

"I don't dislike him. They had a lavish wedding before I left for college last year." I went back for Christmas break.

62

With Henry around, our house doesn't much feel like my home anymore. That's why I interned at NASA this past summer.

"Hey, I'm glad you told us. It's bugged me that you've been so secretive. They're not so bad. Hey, a few of my male relatives have served time in Stringtown." Andi turned and gave my shoulder a squeeze.

"Stringtown?"

"A maximum-security jail on the Oklahoma-Texas border. The Oklahoma branch of our family is crawling with desperados."

"Well, Andi, that makes me feel better." I could safely roll my eyes because Andi had already turned. "Anyway, that's why I want to find the perfect guy. So we can all live a stable, normal, life----eating dinner every night with our two stable, normal kids."

Jane nodded. "I get it. I wish my mom had been my best friend to walk me through high school. I wish she hadn't died when I was nine."

"I hate to sound harsh, but even the best marriages aren't perfect. And in high school, even the most wonderful mother can be a thorn in your side." Andi adjusted her pack. "I know it seems like I had everything. Lots of family. My own daddy is a pain, but my mother and stepfather are crazy about each other. Overall, I had a great childhood. But, believe me, nothing is perfect."

Jane never slowed the pace as we walked. My legs ached. "I'm tired. What about a water break?"

Andi pulled off her boots and flexed her toes. "Is it just me, or is it getting very dark and very cold?"

"Clouds are moving in fast. I hope we'll still have a good view from the top." Jane stared at the sky. "The weather shifts quickly up here."

The terrain changed to rocky ledges. We climbed hand over hand. I had to jam my boot into a crevice and then haul myself up. Jane loosened rocks as she ascended. They rattled down the hill toward us. Moisture covered some of the boulders, making them slippery. Andi moved slowly, appearing to calculate each step.

The fog grew thicker until we could barely see an arm's length ahead. What if we couldn't find our way back down? Would we have to spend a night on the mountain? I stuffed my feelings of panic. I wanted Andi to be the one to act panicky. Being the girlie girl, that should be her role. But Andi remained cool.

We finally reached the base of the tower. By that point, the fog was so thick we could barely see each other, let alone figure out what stood above us.

As we sat on the damp concrete pad between the four steel pillars, I could tell Jane felt rattled. She said, "This is okay. I know it will burn off. We'll find the logging road."

Andi took food out of her pack. "Let's enjoy the ambiance. We're dripping with atmosphere up here. Too bad we're short on guys."

Jane emptied her backpack, too. I felt like a miscreant for not contributing. "Sorry I didn't bring food."

"The pleasure of your company is all we care about." Andi handed me a tuna sandwich.

"Speak for yourself, Andi." Jane gave me some orange slices and bag of carrot sticks. "You get to carry my knapsack down the hill."

We ate slowly. The fog did not seem to be burning off. As Jane stowed trash into her pack, she said, "I wish a forest ranger would show up right now."

Although no rain came down, the thick fog soaked through my light sweatshirt. The chill bit me to the bone.

Andi shivered. "Hey, why don't we start a fire? We can get ourselves nice and toasty."

"We don't have matches." Jane snapped her pack shut.

I dug into the inner pocket of my sweatshirt. Yes! I found a plastic bag with both matches and a joint. "Got matches."

Andi narrowed her eyes. "Why do you have matches? You don't smoke."

"She smokes dope." Jane seemed to get a great deal of pleasure out of making the announcement. Why she chose now, I have no idea. She'd been covering up for me all year, knowing that Andi, who hated drugs of any kind, would pitch a fit.

"Oh my God. Marijuana? Why?"

"To calm me."

"You'd be calmer if you took fewer courses. If you didn't go to every blessed event on campus. If you didn't drink yourself into oblivion every Friday night."

Jane closed her eyes then covered her face. I could tell this conversation did not fit into her idea of how housemates should bond.

"Don't knock it until you've tried it, Andi."

Andi began throwing items into her pack. Then she stopped. "What if I made a deal? What if I smoked that stupid thing—would you promise not to do drugs anymore?"

"What difference does it make to you whether I take drugs?"

"You fool." Andi grabbed my shoulders and shook me. "I care about you."

I thought for a minute. Really, last night was awful. After drinking, I dropped a little mescaline and then vomited for over an hour, hallucinating the whole time. Afterward some slimy guy drove me home.

"Okay. A compromise. No more doing drugs at *frat parties*. But I'm not making any other promises." Smoking dope kept me sane.

"We'll approach your sobriety one step at a time. Jane, aren't there ten steps? Or twelve?"

As I lit up the joint, Jane said, "Is this a national park? This is a felony, right?"

"Nobody is here. And nobody is coming. Why not relax?" I took a toke and handed the joint to Jane who did the same. Andi hesitated, glared at me, and inhaled deeply.

After a few go rounds, Jane said, "Tia, what are you looking for in life anyway?"

"Right now I'd settle for finding the way back to Canaan." I grinned, believing I had made an incredibly profound statement.

I stubbed out the roach. "I am not a nature woman like you, Jane, but in my humble opinion, this fog is thicker than ever. I don't want to spend the night on this damn mountain."

"You are getting on my very last nerve." Andi dug into her backpack. "I have a compass. Let's take a look."

Andi with a compass? My respect for her grew.

Jane and Andi huddled over the map. Cold sober, neither of them had a dependable sense of direction. Being stoned definitely put them at a disadvantage. I was the physics and philosophy major. I should have employed my science and logic skills to figure out a solution, but I had become fascinated by water droplets on a blade of grass.

Ultimately, we started walking on the widest path that led from the concrete pad. Maybe it was the logging road?

It wasn't. As the fog burned off, we found ourselves in a huge meadow.

Jane stopped suddenly and yelled. "Ouch! A bee stung me." As we walked, Jane's whole body seemed to droop. I noticed she began to cough and rub her eyes. "Jane, are your eyes itchy?"

Jane sat down on the path. "Feeling dizzy. Head aches."

"Are you allergic to bees?" What did my first aid manual say about insect stings?

"Don't know. Skin itchy." Jane pointed to her shirt.

She lifted her shirt. Flat red splotches everywhere.

My mind raced: hives, dizziness, weakness, coughing— the symptoms of anaphylactic shock.

She needed epinephrine soon. If I remembered correctly, the next stage was respiratory arrest.

I didn't want to panic Jane, so I took Andi aside. "I think Jane's having an allergic reaction. Run down the path. Listen for road sounds. Flag down somebody."

Andi sped off three times faster than I ever expected.

I strapped on Jane's pack then stooped to support her as she walked. "We've got to keep moving."

Jane leaned hard against me. I noticed red welts on her neck near her collar. "Breathing okay?"

"Chest tight."

About five minutes later, I heard Andi shouting. I yelled back, "Over here."

Andi ran toward us, followed by a woman dressed in a T-shirt and shorts. "This is Ellie. She's got a pickup truck. She can drive us."

Ellie said, "Convenience store is right down the road. You can call an ambulance. Let's lift her." The three of us half dragged, half carried Jane out of the meadow and up onto the road.

Ellie and Andi pulled a kayak out of the bed of the truck. Then I got in. They lifted Jane into my arms. "How is your breathing?"

She shook her head and barely whispered, "Not good."

I wished I could breathe for her. "I'm right here." As if that would be helpful when her throat closed up.

Which other drugs were used with allergic reactions? Antihistamines. Benadryl was an antihistamine, wasn't it?

When we arrived at the store, Ellie hopped out of the cab and ran straight in to make the call. Andi hoisted herself into the truck bed. "How is she?"

"Not great. See if they sell Benadryl. Get the liquid."

Jane had a hard time swallowing but finally got it down. "Does your throat feel swollen?"

Jane nodded and closed her eyes. She started to slump, but I thought she'd breathe better sitting. So I stayed behind her, holding her upright. Her hair smelled like apple blossoms. She'd been poaching my shampoo again. If she survived this, I'd go out and buy her a gallon of the stuff.

Andi took Jane's hand and began speaking softly.

"What are you doing?"

"Praying."

I wish I believed in God, but I don't. Right then, though, I was glad Andi had faith. "See if you can make a deal. Tell God I'll stop screwing around so much."

Andi shook her head. "Doesn't work that way."

I held Jane as we waited. I could feel each shallow, rapid breath she took. Did her lips seem blue? I couldn't tell. The back of her shirt and the front of mine were soaked with sweat. I started to think about how easy it would be for her to die right now--how easy it would be for any one of us to die. I'd always felt invulnerable. I brushed the damp bangs from Jane's forehead.

Jane's eyes opened. "Scared."

Andi squeezed her hand. "God's going to take care of you."

Well, I sure hoped so. I also hoped God's idea of how to take care of Jane coincided with mine.

The rescue squad arrived within a few minutes. One of the workers gave Jane a shot of epinephrine as the other strapped an oxygen mask on her. I rode with Jane in the ambulance. Ellie went back to pick up her kayak. Then she and Andi followed in the truck.

Andi arrived in the ER a little after me. "Where's Jane?"

When I said I wasn't sure, Andi barged right into the patient care area. I followed, wondering if we'd get into trouble.

Andi cornered an orderly. "Got a Jane Holmes in here? Bee sting."

"Curtain three. Are you family? It's family only."

The orderly hadn't finished his sentence before Andi burst into the exam area with me following apologetically behind.

"Is she okay?" Andi asked a nurse who was getting vitals.

The nurse looked up. "Which one of you is Tia?"

I nodded.

"That Benadryl bought her time. Good thinking."

"Will she be all right?" Andi asked.

"She's stable. Sometimes you can have a rebound allergic reaction. We'll keep her here tonight."

Andi jumped onto Jane's cot. "Girl, you scared the daylights out of us." Jane smiled but seemed groggy. Later, we came back with three spoons and a carton of Ben and Jerry's Chunky Monkey ice cream. Jane revived enough to eat half the carton on her own.

* * * *

I wish I could tell you that I've lived the rest of my life cold sober. Not so much. However, I am living more carefully than before. So, that's good.

Maybe Andi is right. Maybe there is a heaven and eternal life is a possibility. But for right now, all I know is that my life is a blip in boundless time and infinite space. My life in this *particular* space and *specific* time is fleeting and a gift.

On the next day, the day Jane left the hospital, I went out and bought her a homecoming gift, a bottle of apple blossom shampoo. Extra large.

Blank as the Minute After Death

Deborah M. Prum

Sweat soaks Ben's yellowed T-shirt in a triangle from his shoulders down to the small of his back. Tension ripples in spasms through tight muscles. Beads of perspiration gather on his forehead and then drip along both sides of his jawline.

He wishes Chester, the lighting guy, would shine the spot away from him. For the last ten minutes, as Ben arranges the set, stacks chairs, picks up debris, the man follows him with the blazing light. This is unnecessary because the improv show isn't even starting for another ten minutes. Maybe Chester is a sadist and secretly loves to make Ben broil. The man never laughs at Ben's scenes. Night after night, Ben glances up, hoping to see a faint smile or a glimmer of light in Chester's eyes. No dice.

Relax. Take a deep breath. Hard to do. The tiny, rundown, theater lacks ventilation. On a hot summer's night like this one, the stagnant air traps odors: fruity perfume, aftershave, cigarette smoke, coffee. Ben's stomach turns.

He burps up the tuna sandwich he'd gobbled down for dinner. The half-sandwich had been in the refrigerator for at least a week.

He regrets eating the tuna, but the only other choice in his empty refrigerator was a jar of capers, tangy capers left from a romantic dinner his girlfriend, Josie, had made on their first date a year ago. Broiled salmon, risotto, a Caprice salad.

At the end of that meal, she cupped his face in her hands and, said, "I adore you." He could smell the salmon, garlic, lemon, and capers on her fingers, but no matter. She loved him. No, she adored him. His heart had filled to bursting.

Ben squints into the house, checking the seats, trying to make out Josie's face. Not there. He looks behind him, at the back of the stage. Ted, Kat, James, Jared, and Marielle, the other members of his improv group, are trailing in.

Lately, Josie and he argue all the time. They bicker about his late nights at the theater and her picnic lunches in

Central Park with Bo, the former boyfriend. They fight about his inability to come up with a rent check and how she also has to pay for food most of the time. Last night they battled about her instructions regarding next week's Christmas party at her office. Josie said, "Ben, don't tell my colleagues you do improv for a living. Improvise another damn career."

Ben stands at the edge of the stage, outside the range of the infernal spotlight, scanning the room. Definitely no Josie. Then he hears his name, more of a hiss than his actual name. He looks back. Off stage, partially behind the curtain, stands Josie. She's gesturing with her index finger, "Come here."

Ben checks his wristwatch. One minute until curtain. He walks over to Josie. His girlfriend says, "It's over. I'm sorry, Ben, you're just not that humorous."

Ben backs away, stumbling on stage, his mind as blank as the minute after death. The tuna does a tap dance in Ben's belly. Oh Lord, don't let me toss dinner on stage.

He feels his pulse, thready and weak. The front of his shirt clings to his chest, drenched and reeking of failure. The dark edges of the small room seem to fold in and out, getting gray and fuzzy around the edges. A wave of nausea sweeps over him. His knees buckle. He leans into the scratchy black curtain along the wall, letting it envelop him. He looks back for Josie. She's already gone.

Ben closes his eyes, tries to steady himself. The director gives the cue. The lights black out. The audience quiets. Ben steps forward. A single beam shines on him, center stage. He can barely utter this sentence, "Welcome to Improv Night at the Eclipse Theater. May I have a word, please?" Ben steps back into the half-circle where five members of his troupe are standing.

Several people shout out words, but the loudest and clearest is "JOY!"

Ben steps into center stage, tears streaming down his face, so many tears that the audience in the last row can see them clearly. He covers his face and bows his head.

Then, tentatively, Kat comes onto stage, a tiny jump in her step. The jump becomes bigger and bigger until she is springing around the stage like Winnie the Pooh's buddy,

Tigger. She smiles at Ben, as she leaps up and down. Soon, Ted enters and matches Kat on the other side of Ben, up and down, up and down.

Ben lifts his head slightly as James and Marielle spring forward from the back of the stage. All four jump around for a while, different heights, different parts of the space. After a while, they encircle Ben, bouncing and grinning, bouncing and grinning. Ben looks at them and can't help but smile. They tap him lightly—head, shoulders, chest. The audience bursts into laughter.

The group gathers closer and lifts Ben at the elbows. At first Ben resists, but then he relaxes into their arms. They all wobble and bounce, and wobble and bounce again. Jared cuts the scene.

Ben laughs, a great gut laugh from the center of his soul. The audience applauds.

Threads

Cathy Herbert

(Second place fiction, Blue Ridge Writers Chapter contest, VWC, 2017)

Seconds after I paid for the oversized artist's paintbrush, I worked out the math. It had cost as much as half a dozen dinners at the Indonesian restaurant down the street. It was a fabulous brush. I could mold it into any shape and it immediately snapped back, all of the coarse bristles perfect and straight. When I rubbed them hard on my palm, they bent in arcs. I would be able to twist the brush hard, gouging the hairs deeply into the canvas surface. Or I could let them glide, leaving a faint thread of color. Or twist the brush in my wrist to leave ribbons of pigment. I could make any mark, any mark in the world.

What would the purchase do to my travel budget? Amsterdam was expensive. I had to factor in the admission price for the Rijksmuseum, the place I most wanted to visit. I calculated against how much money I had for the day. Until tomorrow, I would have to make do with nothing more than a Toblerone chocolate bar and a cup of coffee. I decided to have the coffee immediately, with just a sliver of chocolate. The café, far too dark for morning, smelled like closing time. I took a seat at a window table, swirled the oily liquid, and wondered how old it was. It would be bitter, but that was all right. I bit off a tiny bit of the brown brick of chocolate and let it melt in my mouth. When I drank from my cup, the coffee's acid taste brought out the milky cocoa sweetness. I played with the thread of silver foil wrapping from the chocolate bar, twisting it into a ribbon that glittered as it caught the morning light. It had been raining, but the sky was starting to clear, with patches of sunlight crystalline on the damp, brown paving bricks, reflecting hints of pale blue, yellow, orange, and red. A pink bicycle passed, its reflection shimmering purple and blue in shallow puddles. The rippling water caught the colors in rhythms of motion.

I thought of my mother, her life a shadowy thread, connected to the distant past and, eventually, cut off from the present. Before her mind wandered off completely and never returned, and her body soon followed suit, we played Scrabble every day. Her ancient fingers would tremble, hovering above the Scrabble board. Filtered through the lace curtains, warm patterns of soft light rippled on her blue-veined translucent skin. It was her turn. Just to have something to do, I counted the seconds. I was up to fifteen-one-thousand when she finally gestured toward a row of empty squares. I thought she was about to make a play. Instead, she drew her hand back into a fist, large bony knuckles marked by age spots the color of worn pennies.

"I can't do this anymore."

"Just make a move, any move, it's only a game." I tried not to become impatient.

"I don't remember how to play." She sighed, resigned. Her finger, pointing somewhere out of sight, wavered in the air like a dowsing rod. My mother's brain, a landscape without water, had begun the process of dying years before. I thought of the artist's brush and the marks it could make: faint ribbons of pigment, fading off into nothingness.

For a time, my father hid her decline as effectively as he buried his own reality as a survivor of World War II prison camps. Life is not fair: My mother's recollections of a pleasant life in suburbia faded into nothingness. My father's memories remained as sharp as the blizzards and bayonets of the 1945 death march through Germany. What happened to him is recorded in war crimes documents. Life does not snap back into place, like the bristles of an expensive artist's brush after you gouge it into a painting's surface. I am told that, during his last hours, in hospice after accepting that his condition was hopeless, he slept soundly without medication. A painting of a manicured garden filled with pastel flowers hung over his bed. In all his life, since the war ended sixty-seven years before, he had rarely known a peaceful sleep.

Contemplating her next Scrabble move, my mother bit a fingernail, furtively with small teeth. Her skin had become the color of her beige armchair. When I bought furniture for her, days before she moved into the assisted living facility, the color seemed a festive gold. Finally, it took on the tones of her life. The arms became tattered. For hours, she examined the fabric, trying to pluck out loose threads. She would wrap the long, brown threads around her blueish fingers. She rarely left her room.

In the Rijksmuseum where Rembrandt reigns, I snuck a small square of chocolate into my mouth and tried to examine *The Nightwatch*. I threaded my way through the crowd until I reached the front of the line to see the painting, leaning into the red velvet ropes that draped from rows of stanchions. I wanted a close, careful look at the brushwork and the marks he had made. So many of them, so varied. To see the rhythms of movement made by his arm and hand. The places where the paint hit the canvas surface, hard and determined. Where his moves became delicate and precise. Or tentative and ephemeral, by design. When he made a from-the-shoulder arc in the intersection between intuition and intent. When the world works exactly as you plan. When all the threads connect. I looked for clues about the process of painting in the remnants of color that peeked through at the edges of forms. At a distance, the painting's bodies, costumes, feathers, and swords all seemed so concrete—far more solid than my mother's trembling pale-blue fingers that pulled at brown threads on the armrest of a chair that enfolded her frail body. How did he twist and turn the brush to form these threads of paint? Up close, the objects in the painting—velvet tunics, flashing jewels, weathered flesh—were nothing more than wisps of brush strokes. I wanted to follow the rhythms of this dark painting that rippled with color, caught the light, and reflected it back at me.

I tried to step sideways to follow the rhythms of the brushwork. It was impossible. The pack of closely wedged gallery goers dictated my path. I couldn't follow—with my own movement, my own footsteps—the threads of brushwork, light, and color. I imagined that, in constructing this painting, Rembrandt had always been on the move, forward, backward, going somewhere, coming back, racing, slowing. To follow his steps would be the only way to really see it. Otherwise, I might as well just look at the drab brown poster in the gift shop.

Immobile in her beige chair, my mother stared at the Scrabble tiles. Finally, she hunched forward, almost lurching into the board. "I think this is a word." She was excited—finally, she might have a victory over Alzheimer's. From a tightly closed fist full of Scrabble tiles, she pulled out the squares, one at a time, to spell "liad." One all-important letter landed on a red square. She was triumphant: she would get a triple word score. Although she remembered little of her life, she yearned for triples.

"It'll work." If I corrected her, she would become frustrated and petulant.

"Count it for me." I added up the points.

In the hospital, a few weeks before, she had gulped air through sparse tears and whispered sobs. "Am I dying?"

"No, you just fainted."

"I want to die."

The doctor stood quietly, showing his compassion by offering to do nothing.

"We can run tests," he told me later. "But it won't change the outcome."

"Let it go," I said.

"She doesn't want to live."

"I know."

She was disappointed when an attendant wheeled her into the sunlight, and I drove up to take her back to assisted living. It had been raining. The blue of my car was reflected in the puddles in the driveway.

"I want to go back to Florida."

"OK, if you want to. But it will be a long plane ride."

"I want to be with him."

"Dad's dead."

"I want to be near the cemetery. I want to visit him."

"You have his ashes in your room."

"That's not enough."

What is enough? When dad died, she said she couldn't live. But, two years later, she is still here, plucking at threads in an oversize padded chair. Plucking at threads of a forgotten life.

At the Rijksmuseum, I wandered into a smaller room, empty of tourists but full of small portraits. Surreptitiously, I ate another small square of chocolate. I thought of my father, a World War II POW survivor, who came home, still six feet tall but weighing only 120 pounds. A mass of skin and bones, he was wracked by tuberculosis and pleurisy, having lived for so long on bread made from beet pulp and slivers of sawdust. He always lived, partly, in the threads of the past, in the death march through Germany during an icy winter. His boots had holes in them. His feet were never warm again. He always remembered, even as my mother had forgotten and picked at the armrest of a comfortable beige chair.

I stood in front of a minor work, *Titus in a Monk Habit*. I stared at the figure's brown robes, almost the color of my chocolate bar. But, in a testament to the magic of pigment and light, I saw that the monk's hood really was not brown at all. It was fashioned from restrained brush strokes in muted blue, red, and orange, with a thread of gold highlight to define the knife-edge fold of the peak of the rough brown fabric. I smiled. This device, a threading of bright gold paint against a dark background, often portrays strands of gold chains and the settings for jewels. Yet, the technique works just as well to show the contour of a piece of rough chocolate-brown fabric. The color that defined the edge of the hood at the monk's face shifted—at points I could barely determine—from orange to blue. Small brushstrokes, as precise as the lines in an etching, spaced evenly and effortlessly, angled to describe a physical plane.

When I looked at the front of the monk's habit, rich with bravura strokes, I imagined the painter's movements, the surety of the gesture. Angle your arm just so, shift your wrist like this, and in a flash, the bright colors coalesce to signify heavy brown cloth with a solid figure beneath. The passage of paint that defines Titus's torso, for that moment, seemed to me to contain all the history of painting, extending from the galloping bison of Lascaux painted with pigments derived from the earth to the landscapes of Anselm Kiefer, filled with actual soil and straw.

Just before the death march's end, my father had been left for dead on the side of a road, in the soil of Kiefer's Germany. He was picked up by a farmer, who placed him in a wheelbarrow and took him to a barn filled with soldiers from Canada. They placed him on a straw mat and fed him soup. They saved his life, which had been hanging by a thread.

As I examined Titus, I ate another small square of chocolate, thinking of hunger, longing, and brown dirt on the side of a cold snow-covered road long ago in Germany. The small piece of canvas seemed to contain everything that could be done with a paint brush, every movement, convention, stroke, smudge, meaning, and suggestion. And the threads of memory, real and imagined.

I visited my mother in assisted living every other day, although I never know why. I had never been close to her. I understood her no better at the end of her life than I did when, almost fifty years ago, I moved out of my parents' house, an angry teenager determined to be on my own. I felt no guilt when I didn't visit. Perhaps I spent so much time with her because I saw her most clearly in the tiny threads of life that she remembered and described over and over, always with the same words, mantras that I could recite along with her if I chose to do so. She was not bothered by what she had forgotten, the many decades that no longer existed for her.

On the dark highway, a wisp of a white line threads into the distance. Going somewhere? I was a teenager, and I didn't know. Just away. The threads that held my life together had come undone. I sat, legs spread wide, on the back of the motorcycle, hands wrapped around his stiff leather jacket. We raced up the hill, on the wrong side of the road, unmoored. Too many years ago, too many threads woven tightly and then plucked loose. Light and air, brush strokes and figments. Life formed and unformed, like so many brush strokes, that sometimes gauge into the surface and then fade in a wisp of pigment and light, into the distance.

I ate another small square of chocolate, stared at a painting, thought about cold feet, forgotten memories, and reflections of sunlight in the puddles of Amsterdam.

Journey's End

Gwendolyn Thompson Poole

(Third place fiction, *Skyline* contest, 2017)

Eliza was out of breath when she reached the creek. She had not realized how close she was to the road until she heard hoofbeats and men's voices. She slid down the embankment, hid in the bushes, and watched. Two white men rode along with a bound runaway holding tight to a rope as he trotted along behind their horses. Eliza held her breath and watched this all-too-familiar sight. She didn't recognize the captured man, but she had pity on him, knowing what his likely fate would be. When they were out of earshot, she ran as fast as she could.

Now, sitting by the creek, Eliza was hungry and thirsty, but she knew not to drink from the creek. The rations she packed before leaving the plantation nearly a month ago were long gone. The two biscuits she had gotten from an old couple along the road the previous day were a fleeting memory. Even so, she checked all the pockets of the oversized jacket she wore once again. Empty. Eliza's smooth, dark skin was damp with perspiration. Exhaustion was her immediate enemy. It consumed her now. She must rest.

Eliza woke with a start. She was not sure how long she had slept; it was still dark. Neither was she sure of what had awakened her. There it was again, a movement in the brush on the other side of the creek. Eliza froze, only hearing the pounding of her own heartbeat. If they were Marse Anderson's hounds, surely I would have heard them long before now, she thought, knowing that he would have sent slave catchers after her. Eliza strained in the darkness trying to make out anything in the sparsely wooded area. Then, as her eyes adjusted to the darkness, and with the help of the faint moonlight, she could make out the silhouette of a doe and her fawn peering in her direction. With relief, she slowly extended her hand over the hem of the tattered, old jacket until she could feel the handle of the paring knife she had managed to take from the "Big

House" kitchen when preparing for her escape. Though her moves were slight, they caused the doe and the fawn to skitter away.

Still weary from her journey, Eliza sat up to get her bearings. She removed the soiled head rag and rinsed it in the creek. She worked her fingers through her thick hair to free it from the knot worn beneath the scarf. The cool water from the creek was refreshing to her face and neck as she wiped them with the damp rag.

Eliza had traveled from Caswell County, North Carolina, with her heart and mind set on getting to the North, to freedom. She told no one of her plan to run, not even Rosa who took care of her after her mama and papa were sold away many years ago. It would be better if Rosa knew nothing and Eliza knew that Rosa would make every effort to talk her out of running. Eliza thought of nothing else and decided to make her break in the spring as soon as the planting season was over.

She covered much of the distance on foot, but on a few occasions she accepted rides on false-bottom wagons or practically buried beneath a mound of hay on the back end of a cart. At any rate, she knew she was now well into Virginia, still a far distance from the free soil of Philadelphia and reaching Samuel. She pulled the jacket closer around her and fought back the thought of turning back to Marse Anderson's place. She missed Rosa and the others, missed the singing in the fields, missed the few times of laughter down in the quarters, missed the times they would slip away beyond the tree line for *their* time to pray and worship and singing *their* songs, the ones with the hidden meanings.

I must keep moving, Eliza convinced herself as she gathered her satchel. Must get to the North. She forged ahead, remembering what she had learned about the tree moss, following the North Star, and wading in the water to keep her scent from the dogs. Eliza moved on, ignoring the sounds of the small night creatures and breathed in the smell of the young tobacco plants.

When the sun rose the next morning, Eliza heard hushed voices above her and saw two sets of old work boots standing next to her resting head. As she raised her head and squinted, she saw two men looking down at her. They looked as scared as did she. "You all right, chile?" one tall man around age thirty asked. Eliza sat up quickly, looked around for others, then while keeping her eyes on the two men, slowly ran her hand over the hem of her jacket.

"We don't aims to hurt you none," the shorter, stooped man said, then asked, "You's a runaway?"

"I'm from Caswell County, North Carolina. Where am I?"

The taller man exclaimed, "Chile, you done come all de way from Caswell County by yo'self?"

"Why you's in Andersonville in Buckingham County, Vaginny," the short man offered. "How long you been on de run?"

"Is you hungry, gal? What's yo name? I's Jasper an' dis here's old Peter. We belongs to Massa Scott, Nathaniel Scott. He be de owner of dis here land you be sleeping on."

Peter offered, "Is you hungry? I's sho Miss Irene can find you some vittles. She's de cook for de Plantation. I's sho she can find you somethin'."

"Yes, I'm powerful hungry. I'd be most grateful to you for anything to eat," Eliza said eagerly.

Looking around, Jasper instructed, "Well, you stay right here an' outta sight 'til we comes back. You be safe here 'cause nobody ever come down dis far to de edge of Massa Scott's land."

"Wait here. We be right back." Peter added as they started up the embankment that led them back to the slave quarters.

Eliza stood there, welcoming the gentle rays of the early June sun on her face. She studied her surroundings and thought of the distance ahead of her. "How much longer, Lord, and will I ever see Samuel again?" she whispered. When she realized that the men might not come back, or worse, bring a patroller or overseer back with them, Eliza considered moving on, and quickly. Just as she was gathering her things, she heard, "Psst, gal." She turned, squinted into the sun and saw Jasper and a young woman not much older than her twenty-four years.

"Hi, I'm Rachel like in the Bible. Jasper here's my man. Massa let us jump the broom just last month," she smiled warmly and handed a covered pan to Eliza.

"Thank you kindly, Rachel. My name is Eliza and I'm real hungry," she responded eagerly. "I don't know what it is, but it smells powerful good." The two young women sat as Eliza cleaned the pan of grits, yams, a piece of ham, and a biscuit. Jasper stood holding a jar of tea before his bride took it and handed it to Eliza. Rachel and Jasper watched.

"Miss Irene fixed yo plate and 'spected it was for a runaway, but dint ask no questions, just give me dat look." Rachel and Eliza laughed as Jasper put his hands on his hips and imitated Miss Irene's "look."

"Well, I s'pose I betta be gettin' back up dire foo I be missed and dat ole overseer gets to worryin'. Godspeed, Eliza," Jasper turned and walked away.

"Jasper wants you to rest up for a spell before heading on your way. Keep out of sight, back in that thicket yonder. One of us will come back just before dark to bring a fresh set of clothes and some food for your journey. You must leave when it gets dark. Jasper said you're trying to reach Philadelphia. You're a brave girl, Eliza." Rachael studied her. "You speak well so you'll do fine once you get there."

"The missus from my first plantation was kind to me and taught me to read and write, but what about you? They teach you here?"

"Missus Scott just seemed to take a liking to me when I was young and permitted me to sit in while little Missy Julia had her lessons. She made me promise not to tell anybody, but all the other slaves suspected it. They say I talk like a white person." Rachel chuckled lightly.

"When my husband and I—" Eliza began.

"You're married, Eliza? Where is your husband? Did you leave him behind?" Rachel interrupted.

"Samuel and I got married when we were at the first plantation. We were so happy then. Of course, plantation life was hard because we didn't have our freedom, as you know. That first master had fallen on hard times and couldn't pay his gambling debts. So, he sold off most of his slaves and a lot of other property too. Samuel said that if we don't get sold together, he would run for his freedom and then come back for me."

"Oh, that was so risky. Sometimes they kill runaways or sell them way down South, you know," Rachel added.

"I begged Samuel not to run, but he had been sold to a mean planter from South Carolina. We knew we would never see each other again, so he ran in hopes of getting to Philadelphia, where Quakers, white people, and even some free coloreds would help him. Said he would work and save enough wages to come back and buy my freedom. And if he didn't have the money, he would come back and steal me away from Marse. But, Rachel, it's been more than three years. I couldn't bear to wait any longer so I made up my mind to run when I felt the time was right. Besides, Marse Anderson had started giving me a lot of unwanted attention, if you know what I mean."

Rachel took Eliza's hands in hers. "I pray God's protection over every step of your journey. You'll need it. Get some rest now and one of us will be back before nightfall." Rachel left.

Having a full belly and a weary body made it easy for Eliza to sleep, safely tucked beneath the brush in the thicket at the edge of the Scott plantation. But it was a fitful sleep. She had that dream again, the one about her mother and father. Although Eliza could not see their faces, she knew it was them. The words of the burly slave trader, "Sold away . . . we don't want that little pickaninny!" played over and over in her sleeping mind. Her Mama screamed and hollered. Her Papa didn't say a word, just hung his head in silent defeat as the wagon carried them away. Then her Papa raised his head and whispered her name, "'Liza, 'Liza." When Eliza abruptly opened her eyes and released the clumps of dirt and grass from her fists, she realized Jasper was kneeling beside her, calling her name.

"'Liza, 'Liza. Chile, wake up. You havin' a bad dream. You betta git on up de road while it be good an' dark. We gots a full moon tonight an' dat will be to yo 'vantage." He placed the promised things on the ground beside her. "Here, Miss

Irene packed you somethin' in case you ever find yo'self with dose bloodhounds at yo heels. Dis here is black peppa. Sprinkle some of dis on the ground to cover up de scent of yo footsteps. It confuse dem ole dogs. Dey gits to sneezing from dat peppa an' dey lose yo scent."

Armed with a bundle of yams, biscuits, and a piece of meat, Eliza made her way further north toward Central Virginia. During the next few weeks, she found shelter from a summer shower in a dilapidated old barn on an isolated homestead. One day she slept in the midst of someone's cornfield that sat far from the road and made a meal on the young ears of corn. Eliza traveled mostly at night in order to avoid others along the roads. She wasn't sure how much longer it would take to reach freedom, but she kept in her heart the last words Samuel said to her.

Eliza clearly remembered that night when he stood in the candlelight of their cabin, holding her close. Samuel was strong, with broad shoulders, and stood almost a foot above Eliza's petite five-foot-two frame. He held Eliza at arm's length as if to get one final look at her. He raised his head and whispered fiercely, "God, where are you?" A tear rolled down Eliza's face. Samuel wiped it away. "Don't cry, my queen. I will come back for you one way or another." After a final embrace, Samuel picked up his sack and left the cabin. Eliza stood there for a long moment, then reached for Samuel's jacket on the bench and, in two quick strides reached the door and stepped outside, hoping to catch Samuel. She was too late; he had disappeared into the darkness. Eliza clutched the jacket and breathed in his smell that night as she has done every night since.

"Why are we stopping here, Russell?" asked a white lady with a beautiful green bonnet and a very lacey dress as she sat in a carriage.

"I has to relieve m'self, Ma'am," responded the aged but quick-moving driver as he hurried toward the brush.

"Well, by all means, do so quickly!" she barked with annoyance and continued to fan herself with a lace-gloved hand. Russell moved quickly into the area of overgrowth and was startled when he saw Eliza crouched a few yards away. She held her gaze on him and her breath for fear he might reveal her presence. He moved to another clump of overgrowth to handle his business. "Where are you going now, boy, and what is taking you so long?"

"Thought I saw a rattler in dem bushes yonder, Ma'am. Don't want to git tangled up wit dat thing." Then louder for the benefit of Eliza, "Now you just stay deer, old rattler, 'til wet's gun plum out of sight den you goes on wherever you gots to be gain', you hear?"

"For heaven's sake, Russell, quit carrying on so. You know I have to be at my sister's before sundown. And if I'm not, I'll see to it that you pay for it with your black hide," the lady threatened with all the hatefulness she could muster.

"Yassum, I knows and I'll have you dere in plenty of time. We only gots about twenty more miles to go. Giddy up, you horses! Take us north to the next town!" Russell called to the horses pulling the coach.

Eliza knew that Russell's banter was meant for her ears. She took heed to his warning and stayed low in the bushes for a long time. His message let her know how much further she had to go before reaching the next town. Still a long way from Philadelphia she supposed as she continued her journey.

Feeling a sense of defeat, Eliza stood a few yards from the bank of the wide river and wondered, How am I to get across? As far as she could see, it was wide all the way up and down. Disappointment flooded her fine features as she slumped against a tree facing the setting sun and began to eat the last of the sweet potatoes she had dug from someone's garden the previous day. She softly hummed one of the tunes she recalled from the days on the plantation.

Eliza strained to hear what she thought were voices and realized the voices and movement were getting closer. She stopped humming and froze. The voices and movement ceased also. For what seemed like an eternity to Eliza, there was absolutely no sound save for the gentle ripples of the river. Then Eliza heard a raspy whisper, "Who goes there? Speak up now; I got a weapon." Eliza looked for the jacket to retrieve her knife only to realize that it was just out of reach. "It's a girl, Mr. Benjamin, a young lady," the dark-skinned, older man spoke. Eliza lunged for the jacket when she saw the black man come closer with a white man right behind him. The big man swiftly grabbed Eliza's arm and tossed the jacket to Mr. Benjamin.

She jerked, twisted and kicked him and demanded, "Get your hands off me! Let me go, old man and give me back my jacket!" Then she bit his arm.

"Good Lord, hush yo mouf, gal. We ain't gon hurt you. Quiet now," he ordered and held her firmly with one fleshy hand over her mouth. Once Eliza quieted down, he slowly released her and examined his arm.

The white man advanced, "I'm Mr. Benjamin. Thee must be the runaway from Caswell County, North Carolina, yes? Thee certainly fit the description. Notices are posted all about." Eliza did not answer, but backed away and looked from one man to the other, wondering about their relationship. They did not appear to be slave and master. The white man was wearing one of those funny looking black hats, Eliza noted. Mr. Benjamin answered the question in her eyes. "We can help thee get to freedom. This is my friend, Mr. Adam Wallace. He is a free man now. We are abolitionists," he explained.

Mr. Wallace spoke, "We ran into some patrollers down in Halifax a few weeks ago, said dey been chasing a gal from North Carolina. Seemed real determined to find you and take you back to yo massa. Say dey gon git a real nice price for you long as you not hurt or marked up none. Travelin' by yo'self and 'Liza be yo name, right?"

Looking cautiously at them, she answered firmly, "Eliza, and I want my jacket."

"Well, Eliza, Mr. Wallace and I are traveling north the same as thee and we can help keep thee safe—with thy permission, that is. Thee could be in grave danger traveling alone throughout the countryside, especially with patrollers after thee," he cautioned.

"I thank you kindly, but I'm doing just fine on my own. Got lots of help along the way," Eliza explained as she took the jacket from Mr. Benjamin and began to pick up her bundle.

"Tell me dis den, Miss Eliza. How you 'spect to git 'cross dis here James River? Tell me dat 'cause it's mighty deep and wide." Mr. Wallace grinned.

Eliza looked out as the last of the sun's rays gleamed on the surface of the dull green water. "Okay, just how *we* gonna get across it, Mr. Wallace?" she conceded and smiled.

As the three of them sat near the base of the tree, without mentioning Samuel, Eliza shared with them her plan to make it to Philadelphia, to freedom. She shared with them her desperate attempt to be free of life on the plantation and the advances of Marse Anderson and all that she had experienced along this arduous journey. Mr. Benjamin, who was not more than ten years older that Eliza, had an easygoing, fatherly manner as he explained that shortly after nightfall, if all appeared safe, a lone boatman would come across the river and pick them up. Once on the other side, they would continue northward, stopping at safe houses and points along the way. He and Mr. Wallace were on their way to meet a couple of gentlemen near Charlottesville to pick up a passenger on the Underground Railroad. Eliza was more than welcome to travel with them, but she had to follow their rules explicitly. "It has always been risky business harboring and transporting fugitives," he warned her, "but, even more so now with the amended Fugitive Slave Act."

Mr. Wallace informed Eliza that patrollers and any pro-slavery persons have become more aggressive in their tactics to capture and return runaways. He filled her in on some of the code words used at the safe houses and what to do if they became separated. They had a plan to make the exchange at a meeting place around midnight on a certain mountain. They agreed to have her travel with them to that point at which time they would arrange for her to travel further north with the next abolitionist, who in turn would get her to the next station along the Underground Railroad.

"With prayer and the right connections, thee will likely make it safely on to Philadelphia to meet thy husband. But, be vigilant, as the closer thee gets to the free states, the heavier the patrols are," Mr. Benjamin warned.

When the boat quietly made its way to the river's edge, they climbed aboard and their journey as three had begun. They arrived without incident at a safe house at the base of the mountain just before dawn of the appointed day. Eliza was able to get a bath, such as it was, and put on a fresh set of clothes. She was looking forward to a new life in the North, one that she had only imagined in her wildest dreams. She and Samuel had been separated far too long. In just a matter of weeks, she would feel his embrace and breathe in his essence once again.

After dark, when they got the signal that all was clear, Mr. Wallace, Mr. Benjamin, and Eliza headed up the mountain. She was not sure of the final destination, the two men just referred to it as the top of "The Mountain." She suspected that many a meeting had taken place there, beyond the watchful eye of greedy slave catchers. Traveling in silence and under cover of darkness, the trio reached the appointed meeting place just as Mr. Benjamin and Mr. Wallace had planned. They sat in the darkness and listened. Finally, Eliza whispered, "Where is the man who will take me further North?"

Mr. Benjamin placed a hand gently on her shoulder and replied, "Thee must be patient, my child, we are waiting for the signal."

During their wait, the clouds gradually moved away to reveal a bright, full moon. A sense of peace washed over Eliza and erased her anxiety. She gazed at the moon and the twinkling stars as the nighttime enveloped this glorious mountain and the moon bathed it in its brilliant glow. Eliza felt safe for the first time in her life. With the light of the moon, Eliza could see the valley below this mountain. The land was dotted with a few large farms and a scattering of slave quarters nearby. The light of a random candle flickered then went out. She once again thought of her mama and papa and the people she left behind.

"Won't be long now," came the raspy whisper of Mr. Wallace. "Dat dere's de man what will take you to the North." He and Eliza watched as Mr. Benjamin spoke with the nondescript white man who had emerged from the darkness.

The man retreated into the darkness and Mr. Benjamin approached Eliza and Mr. Wallace. "Now, Eliza, Mr. Peterson will take you on to the next stop. Thee will arrive by tomorrow morning, at which time he will give thee instructions for the journey ahead. Godspeed to thee, my child, Godspeed. Mr. Wallace, you and I have quite a charge before us, a most unusual request. The gentleman with Mr. Peterson is a runaway who has lived and worked in Philadelphia for at least two years but insists on returning to the South to buy his wife's freedom. Our abolitionists in the North tried to dissuade him, but he would not hear of it," Mr. Benjamin continued.

"Once a runaway or freed slave take a notion like dat, he be hell-bent to let nothing git in his way. Oh, 'scuse me, Mr. Benjamin, guess I shudda said dat another way," Mr. Wallace remarked.

"I get your point, Mr. Wallace." Mr. Benjamin placed a hand on his shoulder.

Eliza moved closer to Mr. Benjamin to question him, "Did you say a runaway going back South? To where?"

"A place just across the Virginia boarder, in North Carolina, but Mr. Wallace and I won't have to take him that far. Others will assist him further along his journey," he explained.

Eliza inquired, "What's his name? What does he look like?"

Sensing Eliza's anxiety, Mr. Benjamin said, "Thee need not be afraid, the runaway is traveling south and you will continue on north. Come, Eliza and Mr. Wallace, let us meet Mr. Peterson and make the exchange. It is not safe for us to linger here on this mountain," Mr. Benjamin instructed as he ushered them toward the two approaching men.

At that very moment, Eliza froze and stared, not believing her eyes as the man behind Mr. Peterson stepped from the darkness and into the moonlight. It was Samuel, her Samuel. He looked at her in disbelief, stretched his arms toward her and said, "Eliza, my queen." Eliza's legs became weak as she stood and stared. Then she moved to his outstretched arms and received his warm embrace. Mr. Wallace and Mr. Benjamin stood in awe of this site.

When Eliza looked up at him, a single tear ran down her cheek. Samuel wiped it away and said, "I promised I'd come back to get you one way or another."

Wrapped in Samuel's tattered, well-worn jacket and his embrace, Eliza looked up at the dark sky with its bright moon and stars and whispered, "Samuel, I will forever remember our nighttime on the mountain. Now, let's go north to freedom. Let's go home."

The Succession

Valerie B. Williams

(Third place fiction, Blue Ridge Writers Chapter contest, VWC, 2017)

Cleo knelt in front of the weed, wrapped her hand around it, and yanked. Her fingers slid up the plant, stripping all the prickly leaves but leaving the stalk firmly in the ground.

"Dammit," she said and sucked on her sore index finger.

"I'm gonna win, you bitch." She used both hands on the stalk and leaned away from the weed until the taproot gave up its grip, bringing up a large clump of clay and toppling her onto her butt. Weeds clung to soil like limpets to rocks. Or certain people to prizes. She wiped a hand across her sweaty forehead, leaving a smear of soil and a little blood.

Her satisfaction was short-lived, however, when she looked at her garden. Ten tomato plants were lined up in two rows of five, spaced six feet apart and enclosed by tall, square cages. All heirlooms, or at least potential heirlooms. Right now they had shriveled leaves, and a few of the fruits had blossom-end rot. Some of the plants had no fruit at all, not even green.

A buzzing sound to her left, like a hummingbird, startled her. She turned to see a tiny, pale woman hovering at eye level. The woman was about six inches tall and wore a light-green toga. She had long, fine, white hair and a youthful face, with dazzling emerald eyes. Her smile displayed a mouthful of pointy little teeth.

"Orrla," said Cleo, relieved. She glanced toward the house. They were alone. "Boy am I glad to see you." She gestured at her garden. "Look at them." Tears of frustration welled.

Orrla flew to the nearest tomato plant, a Brandywine, folded her gossamer wings, and sat on its upper branches with her legs dangling. She glanced down the row of plants and shook her head. A frown wrinkled her forehead when she met Cleo's eyes.

"I've weeded, I've watered, I've fertilized. I've done everything humanly possible. Help," said Cleo.

"It's okay, Klee O," said Orrla. "I will help them." Her voice was musical; she almost sang her words. She flew around each plant, touching the fruit and stroking the leaves. Then she landed and moved between them, sprinkling a sparkly red substance around the roots that shimmered on top of the soil for a few seconds before being absorbed.

Orrla flew straight up and hovered in front of Cleo. She curtsied in midair. "All done," she said with a smile.

"Thank you so much," said Cleo. "Again. I don't know what I'd do without you." She swept her hand toward the plants. "They look better already."

Orrla's eyes caught Cleo's still-bleeding index finger. and she slid her small tongue around her lips. "You're hurt," she said. "Let me help." She flew closer.

Cleo clenched her hand into a fist and covered it with the other hand. "No really, you've done so much already. I . . . I'll be fine."

"Okay, if you're sure," said the pixie, hovering for an extra few seconds before she sighed and flew into the woods.

* * * *

Cleo shuffled back to the house, thinking that Orrla always showed up just when Cleo was desperate. She appreciated the help at the time. The second thoughts came later.

Her arthritic knees ached, aggravated by the extra thirty pounds she was carrying. But, at sixty-three years old, she wasn't about to give up her comfort foods. She loved her nightly bowl of ice cream and her full-sugar sodas. And she kept a supply of chocolates in the kitchen drawer.

She'd always been chubby and mostly ordinary-looking: medium brown hair, medium brown eyes, of medium height. Two characteristics were not medium—her shapely legs (still shapely, even with the extra weight) and (unfortunately offsetting the legs) an oversized bulbous nose. It was as though she'd been assembled from spare parts.

After her mother died, Cleo legally shortened her name from the optimistic "Cleopatra" and joined a dating service. She was looking for a kind, intelligent man—looks unimportant. Unfortunately, it seemed no men considered looks unimportant. She dug into her work, knowing she would have to take care of herself.

She'd retired three years earlier from a long career as a bookkeeper with the transportation department of the Hadley County Schools. She had savings enough to supplement her government pension and maintain a comfortable lifestyle. Gardening was a means to save money on groceries, and she was good at it. When she decided on a whim to enter some of her produce in a contest (and won), she discovered a fierce competitive streak.

She planned to enter her current crop of heirloom tomatoes at the Hadley County Agricultural Fair. Not only was there a small cash prize, but the win also came with a title—Tomato Queen (or King). This was her third year, and she'd come close last year with an honorable mention. She was determined to seize both title and bragging rights this year.

* * * *

She'd just finished feeding Eddie, her medium-size brown mutt, when she heard a knock followed by the creak of the front door swinging open.

"Yoo hoo, it's just me."

"Hi, Barb. In the kitchen," she called, reminding herself to lock the door.

Her neighbor bustled in carrying a large glass platter. A layer cake with white icing perched in the center of it.

"I'm returning your platter, but I brought a cake with it to say thanks. It's your favorite, spice cake," said Barb. She sat the heavy platter on the table and herself in a chair, wincing and shifting to the right before leaning against the backrest. "So, been out in the garden?" She gestured at her own perfectly made-up forehead and pointed at Cleo.

Cleo grabbed a paper towel, wet it, and scrubbed the garden soil off her forehead. "Thanks," she said with a smile.

"Those tomatoes don't grow themselves. At least not the prize-winning ones."

"Don't I know it," said Barb. "I'm out there every day. But it's *so* worth it to win the crown at the fair." She was the reigning Tomato Queen and had won the last two years in a row.

"Well, I wouldn't know about that," said Cleo. Out there every day, my ass. The woman isn't even sweaty, perfect manicure as usual. She *had* to have paid help.

"I'm sure you'll win, eventually. Your tomatoes are always so beautiful," said Barb, with a saccharine smile. "But I'll give you a run for your money." Eddie snuffled at her lap and she scooted to the right, resting both hands on the table. She had cats. Lots of them.

"You enjoy the cake, hon, I've got to scamper," Barb said, pushing herself up from the chair. "Toodles!" The door slammed behind her.

Cleo waited a minute. Then she locked the door and turned to see the dog watching her with his ears perked up. Well, one ear perked up. The other stuck straight out to the side.

"She only wins because she's younger than me," said Cleo. "Isn't that right, Eddie?"

Eddie thumped his tail in agreement.

"That's okay, boy. This year we have a secret weapon."

Thump, thump.

* * * *

Cleo met Barb four years before she retired, when her husband, Andrew, replaced Cleo's longtime boss, Frank. At Frank's going-away luncheon, Barb kept her adoring gaze on her husband, like a wannabe Nancy Reagan. Even worse, she never held a job and her life revolved around him. She picked at her food, claiming she wasn't hungry. Cleo cleaned her plate and finished with two pieces of chocolate cake.

Despite their differences, Cleo and Barb developed a casual friendship. Cleo appreciated Barb's wicked sense of humor, and they met for lunch every month or so. They made quite the odd couple, as Barb was petite, pretty, and stylish. She also was insecure, always asking about the latest college interns and how much time her husband spent with them. Cleo secretly thought part of the reason Barb liked her was that she posed no threat.

When Andrew died of a heart attack the year Cleo retired, Barb was shattered and leaned heavily on her. They'd had no children and Barb had no family living in the area. Cleo tried to be supportive, but she found such neediness foreign and a bit oppressive. After all, she'd been alone since her mother died. Fortunately, after a few months Barb regained her bearings and Cleo was relieved to see less of her. Cleo's life returned to its normal, quiet routine. Until two years ago.

The old Henson place had been on the market for some time with no takers. Barb, who'd always lived in town, decided she wanted to try the country life and bought the house. Two doors down from Cleo. She'd respected boundaries, for the most part, and Cleo had to admit it was nice to talk to someone other than Eddie.

Despite her lack of gardening experience, Barb had won the Tomato Queen title right out of the gate. Twice. Cleo tried to jolly her out of the secret to her success.

"A lady never tells," Barb said, wagging her finger.

* * * *

Cleo pulled off her sweaty gardening clothes. She hissed with pain when she removed her bra, avoiding the three small Band-Aids that surrounded her left nipple. In the shower, she peeled them off and carefully cleaned each dime-size wound. After she had dried herself, she looked longingly at the box of Band-Aids but left the wounds uncovered.

Naked, she walked to her bedroom, opened the window, and slid between the sheets. Her heart raced with dread. She was tired from the day, though, and sleep overtook her within minutes.

A tug on the side of her left breast pulled her out of a dream. She heard the buzzing of small wings and opened her eyes. The sheet was pulled down to her waist and she watched while Orrla applied her pointy teeth, tore off a small chunk of skin and chewed vigorously. Cleo could neither move nor feel pain because of the paralyzing and anesthetic effect of the pixie's saliva. She closed her eyes and waited for it to be over, oddly disconnected from her own body.

She'd first met Orrla last fall, while walking with Eddie. She had just passed the old oak tree when he trotted out of the woods and dropped a pale creature at her feet. She thought it might be an albino squirrel. She bent for a closer look, took off her glasses, rubbed them with her T-shirt, and looked again. It was slippery from dog slobber, but there were no obvious injuries. It was female, and exquisitely beautiful.

The creature introduced herself as Orrla and told Cleo that Eddie had saved her from a hungry fox. She recuperated in Cleo's house for two days, consumed an amazing amount of fresh vegetables and fruits for one so small, and educated Cleo about her kind. Pixies form tribes, she said, and each tribe cares for a specific area of land, ensuring that the vegetation is healthy and productive. Orrla was the leader of her tribe. When the pixie asked how she could repay Cleo for her kindness, all Cleo could think of was next year's fair. And "Queen" Barb.

A small tongue lapping the new wound returned her to the present. The lapping stopped and Cleo opened her eyes, hoping the pixie was gone. Orrla moved to one of the existing wounds and scraped the scab off, causing it to seep. Cleo closed her eyes again and felt Orrla lapping the old sore. She revisited each existing wound and continued to feed. The feeding stopped and Cleo heard the buzzing of wings and felt a faint breeze on her face.

"Klee O," sang Orrla.

Cleo opened her eyes. Orrla hovered in front of her. Her pale skin had taken on a rosy tone. She was terrifyingly beautiful.

"You will win the crown," said Orrla. She flashed a blood-tinged smile and flew out the window.

After a few moments, Cleo wiggled her fingers and toes, testing her ability to move again. She felt faintly nauseated, as she always did after Orrla fed. Once she'd cleaned and bandaged the wounds, though, visions of lush green plants weighed down with perfect fruit flooded her thoughts and brought a smile. Winning the title would make her sacrifice worthwhile.

* * * *

The next day the garden was transformed. The tomato plants were thriving. There were more immature fruits on each plant than yesterday, and the ripe ones were larger and more luscious. Cleo clapped her hands, squealed when she accidentally hit her sore left breast, and then laughed. Between the antiseptic ointment and the sight of her perfect tomato plants, the pain was nearly forgotten.

When Cleo had first asked for Orrla's help, the pixie had explained that she could make Cleo's garden produce healthy, ordinary tomatoes. But she could do more, if Cleo wished. Exceptional tomatoes were possible, but the process depleted her energy and required special food.

Cleo had been horrified at the cost and could never imagine agreeing to that price. But in the spring, after she planted her seedlings, disaster struck in the form of a fungus. She started over, only to have beetles attack. At the height of her frustration, Orrla appeared and offered to help. Cleo gave in. But only under the condition that her "payments" to Orrla be in an area hidden by clothing.

* * * *

Cleo put the finishing touches on her artistic display and stood back to admire her handiwork. The lush ripeness of the fruits and the variety of their colors—pink, red, yellow, purple—were gorgeous. She waited until just before the judging to slice one of each variety and plate them in front of the basket of whole fruits. She leaned over the glistening slices and breathed in their sweet, tangy aroma. She knew the taste was heavenly. It had taken two more visits from Orrla, but these tomatoes were perfect.

"Yoo hoo!" Barb was heading straight for her, favoring her left leg. She wore a hunter green, color-coordinated pantsuit. The dark color made her look more pale than usual.

Cleo forced a smile. "Barb! Did you pull a muscle?" Maybe she *did* actually do some work in the garden. Nails are still perfect though.

"Oh no, just a little stiffness. I'll be fine." Barb stopped in front of Cleo's table and leaned against it.

"Today's the big day. Are you ready?" said Cleo.

"Of course! I just had to see how yours turned out." Barb looked at the fruit, running her fingers lightly across their skin and hmm hmming. "Lovely, Cleo. You've outdone yourself." She put out her hand. "Good luck. I think it'll be close this year."

"Good luck to you as well. As if you need it," Cleo said with a fleeting smile. She rounded the table and looped her arm through her neighbor's. "It's only fair I get to see yours too."

As they approached Barb's table, it was obvious who the real competitors were. All the other displays of tomatoes were average at best. The two standouts were Cleo and Barb.

"Beautiful, Barb. We can both be proud of our hard work." Cleo knew *she'd* worked hard.

Barb sank into a chair behind her table, closed her eyes, and pinched the bridge of her nose. She looked up with a weak smile. "Well, I for one will be glad when it's over. This season has really taken it out of me." She straightened in her chair and patted her perfectly styled (and dyed) hair. "This may well be my last year competing. I don't know how *you* keep going, Cleo."

"Just tough stock, I suppose." Bitch.

* * * *

Peggy Thrasher, the head judge, strode toward Cleo. "Please bring your display to the front table," she said. She pivoted and walked away without looking back.

Cleo balanced her basket and plate and trailed in Mrs. Thrasher's wake. Barb was already at the front table with her wares displayed.

"We're the finalists! Isn't it exciting?" Barb beamed.

"Yes, it is," said Cleo, twisting her sweaty hands together. She felt light-headed.

They stood side by side behind their displays as Mrs. Thrasher conferred with the other two judges. Barb grabbed Cleo's hand. Cleo took deep breaths and watched the judges. Mrs. Thrasher frowned and shook her head. All three came back for another look and then stepped away again. The two other judges seemed to be making an argument to the head judge, who finally sighed and nodded.

Mrs. Thrasher stood in front of the table, hands clasped at her ample waist. One judge stood next to her with ribbon and sash in hand. The other judge jogged up with a matching ribbon and sash.

Cleo's stomach sank.

"This has never happened before," began Mrs. Thrasher, "but we can't decide. You both have such perfect tomatoes." She waved the other two judges forward.

Cleo watched in disbelief as a blue ribbon was placed on each display. She lifted her numb arms to allow the judge to put a sash around her, wincing when the woman bumped her left side. The other judge put a sash around Barb. Both sashes had a picture of a golden crown, followed by the year.

She pasted on a smile while silently screaming, No! I don't want to share.

* * * *

Cleo pulled the newspaper from the box and glared at the front page as she trudged back to the house. There with their arms around each other, smiles frozen in place, were Cleo and Barb, the co-Tomato Queens of the county fair.

She was almost to her front door, still fuming, when she did an about-face and strode down the street. She was going to have a little chat with Barb and find out exactly how she got her results.

Cleo rapped her knuckles against her neighbor's front door, not noticing it was unlatched until it swung inward. "Barb?"

A cat purred and wrapped itself around her legs as she hesitated in the silent hallway. Barb always had the TV or radio or some noise going. Kept her company she said. A clock ticked.

Another cat perched in the doorway to the kitchen, licking its paws. A trail of dark paw prints led down the hall toward the bedroom. Cleo frowned and peeked into the kitchen. Empty. The bedroom door was slightly ajar. A third cat sprinted out of her way with a yowl as she pushed the door open.

A metallic smell hit her nostrils, pushed by the breeze lifting the curtains from the open window. Barb lay naked and face-down on top of the covers, motionless. Something on the lower half of her body was moving. Cleo flipped the light switch and froze. A swarm of pixies pushed at each other like nursing puppies, heads down and buried in Barb's left buttock. Blood covered the tiny bodies, turning them from white to red. Another pair of pixies was working on her right calf. The toes on her left foot were gone. The darkened sheets told of more injuries not visible.

Cleo remembered Barb's limp. And her pallor.

"Orrla?" Her voice shook as shivers racked her body. She swallowed repeatedly, trying not to throw up.

A crimson figure flew up from the scrum. Red droplets from her wings sprayed Cleo's face.

"Queen Klee O," sang the pixie queen. Orrla seemed delighted welcome her to the sisterhood, displaying her bloodstained teeth in a wide grin.

Cleo fled.

* * * *

She locked her front and back doors, and closed all the windows. Her left breast throbbed. She sat trembling at the kitchen table, Eddie watching her with his ears perked up.

Think, Cleo, think!

If they drove far enough, they would be out of the pixies' territory. But this was her home; she couldn't just leave and not come back.

Buzzing sounded from the hallway. Orrla flew in, followed by four of her tribe. Their bodies had turned from red to black. The chimney!

"Queen Klee O," sang Orrla. "We mean you no harm."

"What about Barb?" Cleo picked up Eddie and backed into a corner.

"She broke the agreement. She was punished." Orrla's green eyes glimmered in her black face. "You won!" The pixie looked puzzled.

Horror, happiness, and fear waltzed around her mind. What had Barb done wrong? Cleo had meticulously upheld *her* end of the agreement (she believed). She swallowed hard.

"Thank you," Cleo said, just wanting them to leave. "I'm grateful."

Orrla clapped her tiny hands. "Good. See you next year." The dark cloud of pixies followed their queen out of the room.

Cleo's legs failed and she slid down the wall, holding Eddie in her lap. She would enjoy her reign, but the price had been too high. She would politely decline to continue next year.

If Queen Orrla would allow it.

A Terrible Beauty

Phyllis A. Duncan

At this time of year the difference in temperature at night on the mountain was a welcome respite. Away from the heat-generating asphalt and breezes swallowed by the valley, you could feel as if you were in another world. The stars and the lights of residences merged at the horizon and infused the air with magic.

She could feel it as she climbed. Only at night did magic emerge from the mountain to dance around her and make her hackles rise.

In her arms the animal wriggled, almost flinging itself from her grip. Maybe it suspected its fate.

"Shh," she murmured, stroking it. "It's a little adventure is all, and you have an important part to play. I can't do it without you."

The animal quieted down, and she saw its trusting eyes in the starlight. No, it was "the animal" now, no longer a pet, and she silently asked forgiveness for what she was about to do.

In the clearing at the knoll's crest, she checked the position of the moon and the constellations. The time had to be right. She could bring no machinery here, and her watch was at home. Here, for this, she could only have natural things. Her slippers were calfskin, her shift pure white cotton, the blade she carried flint. The silver bracelet passed down from mother to daughter in her family was acceptable; in fact, it was critical. There hadn't been a single break in that transition for more centuries than anyone could count. The women in her family knew how to ensure the birth of a daughter.

That was why she was here.

She turned her face up to the sky. Perseids flashed above her, so swift she could never be sure she saw them. She checked the position of Pegasus, Andromeda, Pisces.

It was midnight.

She knelt on the damp grass, held the animal down by its neck, and used the flint to slice it open from gullet to genitals. The sound it made was like nothing she'd ever heard before, but the animal soon stilled. She sat back on her haunches and waited for its blood to soak into the ground. The animal had been small, and the smell of offal wasn't disturbing. She'd be long gone before the scavengers came to investigate.

She lay her hands in the cooling blood, stood, and raised her arms skyward, palms uplifted. She murmured a chant uttered by throats cut by the Romans in oaken groves, words also passed from mother to daughters, words men's ears couldn't hear nor men's tongues voice. Starlight glinted off the silver bracelet as the air moved around her, her shift billowing like a cloud.

Midway through the chant, the bracelet glowed, a faint red at first outlining the center of the triskele engraved on it. The glow spread, turning from red to yellow until it seemed as if she wore a circlet of lava on her wrist. She slipped the bracelet free and lay it atop where the blood had soaked into the earth.

The words came faster now, almost beyond the human capability of speech, but she didn't miss a syllable. When she finished, she stepped away, arms lowering to her sides, her eyes fixed on the glowing bracelet.

The air rushed away, as if into a vacuum, and the bracelet rose one foot, two feet, three, a dozen off the ground, spinning and tumbling so fast it was a golden blur. The Perseids stopped in transit. The stars ceased to twinkle. Time had stopped, not long enough to cause any harm, and, in truth, it had stopped only here in the clearing. No one would notice.

The blood-soaked ground pushed upward, creating a small mound. The animal, having served its purpose, rolled away as the mound grew, dirt burbling away in clots. Light from the whirling bracelet shone on a tip of metal, which pushed it way upward until it was obvious it was a sword. The guard emerged, then a pale hand holding the grip, then an arm, a head, a chest, and on until a woman stood there, sword upraised, shield protecting her torso.

The bracelet stopped spinning, hung in the air for a moment, then dropped at the feet of its owner. She picked it up and slipped it back on her wrist.

"You summoned me," the goddess said. The sibilant voice circled the clearing to reach the other's ears.

This goddess didn't require obeisance, and the other stood, head high. She held up her arm so the goddess could see the bracelet.

"Yes. I know your line," the goddess said. "What is your request?"

"I carry a child."

The goddess fixed her gaze on the other's abdomen. "I can see."

"The physicians of this realm have examined me. It is male."

The goddess' eyes glowed as she viewed the other's body. "After this one child, there will be no others."

"Yes. That is what the physicians have told me."

"You ask for the revision."

"Yes."

The goddess looked at the other's abdomen again. "You have waited too long. The gender is set. Your line will end."

"And your power is great, enhanced by the blood and the night and this mountain."

"This mountain is old and has much magic. The blood was strong because the animal was beloved to you, but the result may not be as it should be. It could be a terrible beauty."

"My line is at stake. We must try."

"Womankind would be diminished if we lost your line. Try we must."

The goddess floated to the other and touched the tip of her sword above the other's navel. The other closed her eyes, and warmth spread from her navel, down to her feet, up to her head. The sword glowed much as the bracelet had, thin barbs of lightning coruscating from it. The lightning traveled into the other's body, and she gasped as if she walked across a carpet in winter and gotten "zapped" by static electricity. The other breathed deeply, smelling ozone.

When she opened her eyes, the goddess was gone; the earth as if nothing had disturbed it, the animal's body nowhere to be seen.

* * * *

As the weeks flew by, Emer Joyce grew more despondent with each ultrasound. The child was healthy but still a boy, to her husband's delight, a delight she pretended to share.

And she called her mother. Daily, sometimes once an hour, until Dervia Joyce said, "The goddess works in her own way. You have to trust her."

Emer thought about another summoning, but her husband would question the loss of a second cat so soon after the first.

Emer held out hope up to the moment of birth, up to the point where the doctor said, "A fine, beautiful boy." Everyone thought her tears were ones of joy. When a nurse handed Emer her son, Emer thought the little blue cap looked wrong. Even the baby seemed to dislike it, stopping his fretting only after Emer removed it.

Shannon Joyce *was* a beautiful little boy. Emer had to admit that. Every baby had blue eyes at birth, so her mother-in-law declared, but Emer looked into eyes like her own, surrounded by lush, blond lashes. Everyone remarked about Shannon's hair, fine and blond and long for a newborn. Shannon's fingers and toes were slender and delicate, and as long as Emer didn't look under Shannon's diaper, she could almost see the daughter she would never have.

They brought Shannon home, and Emer thought it strange Dervia was happy with a grandson. Dervia had no other daughters, only Emer's younger brother, but the tradition went from mother to daughter.

Every time Emer apologized to her mother for the end of her ancient and powerful line, Dervia would say, "The goddess works in her own way. You have to trust her."

Shannon was loved, and by his mother most of all. Emer came from a long line of powerful women, but men were always part of their lives—indeed a necessary part. As much as Emer loved her son, she still longed for her never-to-be-born daughter.

As Shannon grew, Emer's husband worried about the size of the child's genitals. They seemed to stay infant-sized as Shannon came to one year, two, three. Doctors explained that all babies developed differently and that, at puberty, Shannon's penis and testicles would catch up with the rest of his body. Emer thought Shannon's genitals grew smaller but decided that was simply because his body grew larger.

Unfortunately, Emer had made a poor choice in a husband. Shannon's genitalia became his obsession, and he took the growing child from doctor to specialist, wanting his son to be "cured," to be a man. Perhaps in her husband's line of men, penis size was important, but Emer finally put her foot down. No more doctors for a healthy child. Shannon would grow in his own way.

Not long after, Emer's husband left, because, he said, "Shannon will never be a man," and Emer found she didn't miss him. Nor did Shannon. Emer's husband apparently didn't miss either of them. He didn't even ask for visitation.

At every milestone of his growth and development, Emer loved her son even more but still saw that never-to-be-born daughter. And Dervia Joyce would say, "The goddess works in her own way . . ."

"I trusted her," Emer said, "but she failed me. I have a son, a son I love, but I can't tell him about our line. I can't teach him the words. He'll never be able to speak them."

And Dervia had smiled and said, "It never hurts to try."

Emer told Shannon about their line but made it sound like a fairy tale. He loved the story and would ask for it again and again. Emer taught him a few of the words, the ones that had found their way into common language. They were difficult for him at first, but he got better at them as he grew older.

Dervia spent hours with Shannon, too, where they took long walks and discussed the things a grandmother and grandchild did, secrets they knew each other would keep. Emer loved to see them together, but sometimes sadness would overcome her. Her mother would die knowing her line would end.

"I should have done the summoning sooner," Emer told her mother one day. "As soon as I did the pregnancy test. I should have done it then."

"The goddess works—"

"Don't say that anymore, Mother. You've said it a hundred, a thousand times, and it changes nothing."

"You have to trust her."

* ** *

Two days before his tenth birthday, Shannon came to his mother and told her he wanted to surprise her.

"But it's the other way around, love," Emer said. "I'm supposed to surprise you."

"Oh, you can, but I want to surprise you, too."

He'd spent a great deal of time with Dervia in the week before his birthday, and Emer knew the two of them were cooking something up.

"Also," he said, "I want to change my name to Shannon Joyce. Why should I still have my father's name when he decided he's not my father."

"Good point," Emer said, "but your grandparents . . ."

"I don't think they'll mind."

True, Shannon's visits to them, weekly at first, had slipped to monthly, quarterly, and now were only once or twice a year.

"If that's what you want, Shannon," Emer said, "we'll do what it takes to change it."

Shannon smiled at his mother. "Good."

* * * *

On the day of Shannon's birthday, he and Dervia sent Emer away for the morning, and when she returned at lunch, she saw Dervia had prepared Emer's favorite foods. The birthday cake was Emer's favorite, chocolate with strawberry icing, and the house was filled with Emer's favorite flowers, pink roses.

"What's all this?" Emer asked her mother.

"Part of Shannon's surprise."

"Today is supposed to be about him, not me."

"You're the mother. It's about you as well," Dervia said. "It's about the whole line of Joyce women, all the way back to when we tamed fire and grew the first grain."

Emer's vision blurred with tears. "And that all ends with me, and don't tell me to trust the goddess."

Dervia smiled and said, "Let me go see if Shannon is ready."

Emer sat on the family room sofa, surrounded by the scent of flowers, and it all came back to her. The trek up the mountain, calming the poor terrified cat, the goddess' pale face, the glow of the silver bracelet as it defied gravity, how time stood still at midnight.

Emer gasped. The bracelet had moved on her arm, and she looked at it. Tiny streaks of lightning danced along its circumference, and Emer found herself back in the clearing, watching as the goddess touched the mound of her stomach with the tip of a sword. The goddess' voice swirled around the room.

"A terrible beauty is born."

Emer stood and looked at the stairs. Dervia came down, Shannon's hand in hers.

Shannon. Beautiful, beautiful Shannon. In a pink dress and gold sandals. With polish on her toes and fingernails. With a little girl's tiara on her head. A little girl's smile on her face. Shannon, the never-to-be-born daughter now born. In terrible beauty.

The goddess works in her own way.

Team Leader

Wendi Dass

Early-morning rays peek over Richmond's downtown. Glass prisms etch the skyline like a three-dimensional jigsaw puzzle, with Commonwealth Power boasting the largest piece. I stretch a long yawn and shield my eyes from the harsh light. Mid-summer dew dampens my brow; my feet are already sweating. I crouch and loosen the laces on my running shoes. Shimmery, reflective arcs. Bright pink laces. I've never bought a pair this loud before. Mine are so much cuter than the blue pair Jill bought.

I stand and search the crowd. No Jill.

I whip my cell-phone from my snazzy new armband and type.

Where r u?

This race was her idea. Her idea to make a good impression. Her idea to skyrocket our college dropout careers as peon associates to team leaders.

Team leader. Did I just get dizzy? Because I should. Snazzy title, enough pay so I can afford my own place, and a chance to rub shoulders with . . . my eyes drift to the front of the mass. He's easy to spot because he's six-foot-four. Massive shoulders. Wavy dark hair. Dane. Office heartthrob and highest TCH performer. What's TCH? I'm sure I'll find out when I become a team leader.

A hand smacks my shoulder. "Thanks for coming out, Ashley."

"It's Amber." I correct Mr. Palmer, team captain, maker of teamer leaders. I flash a smile.

"Amber. Right, right. Don't forget to pick up your goodie bag." He gestures to his shirt. "Group shot after!"

"What a great idea, Mr. Palmer! I can't wait to make that my screensaver."

He winks. "That's the attitude, Abby. You'll be processing TCH reports before you know it."

"Amber!" I call after him, but Mr. Palmer doesn't turn. He jogs toward the starting line.

So much for making a good impression. Jackass doesn't even remember my name.

My phone dances to a Beyoncé beat. Jill! I push the phone to my ear.

"I'm two car lengths from the front." I thrust my hand in the air. "Do you see me?"

A growl louder than Mr. Palmer's morning "Go team!" rushes the line. "Not gonna make it."

I jerk my shoulders back so fast I think my sports bra might suffocate me. "Not coming? But we've trained for this for two months. I spent half my paycheck on these shoes!"

My voice is louder than I anticipated. Mr. Palmer turns and glares at me. I shrink and turn away.

"Two passes around the block doesn't exactly count as training," Jill says.

I chew my lip and bite back my smart-ass comment. This was *her* idea.

"Sorry, Amber," Jill says. "I'm wasted."

"Wasted!" I lower my voice. "But this is *our* chance. Mr. Palmer is here and so is," my voice sweetens, "Dane."

"The guy that looks like Ewan Mc-something-or-other?"

"Yes! So, are you coming?"

Jill gags.

"Places!" someone hollers through a megaphone. "Five minutes!"

Hacking continues on the line. My stomach sinks. Oh God. Jill's puking and the race starts in five minutes. I lower the phone. Five minutes! There's no way in hell Jill will get here in time.

"Amber?" a voice behind me says.

I turn. Phyllis—Grandma Phyllis, as she's known around Team Palmer.

"Phyllis!"

She wraps her thick arms around me, and her plump cheek smooshes into my bare shoulder. My stomach settles.

"I didn't know you were coming." Phyllis pulls back. "Where's your friend? Jill, right? That girl's stuck to you like molasses on biscuits."

I dig my nails into my spandex and force a smile. "She's not going to make it, but I'll be okay. How about you? I didn't think you'd be running."

Phyllis shrugs, her wrinkled jowls meeting her company-logo shirt. "It's my first 5K, but I've been training hard."

I scrunch a smile. If Phyllis can do it, I can do it.

"Faster runners to the front!" the announcer calls.

Phyllis rolls her eyes. "That's my cue. Gotta move to the back."

I give her a consolation pat on the back. She plods through the crowd.

I survey the swarm of sticky racers and join a group that appears to be about my age. They all look pretty fit—but whatever, my skinny ass will keep up.

The race starts and for the first mile I soar. It's like high school gym class except—wait—we should keep running? A cramp jabs my ribs. Shoulders brush against mine as the ponytails of my barely sweating coworkers continue to swing. I teeter to a walk.

Where's the water station? Better, a bench?

I scan the sidewalks. Parking meters. Dark storefronts. Beyond, the leaders circle back and there's Dane. My side-stitch knifes me, but I drag my feet to a sprinter's pace and whiz by the bobbing heads in front of me.

Our paths meet, and am I imagining it, or does he just glance at me? Dare I chance a second look?

I can't help myself. I tip my head over my shoulder. Dane's hair flounces under his quick pace. His calf muscles flex as his feet strike the pavement. His biceps bulge.

Something slams my shoulder.

"Watch it, Amy!" Mr. Palmer shouts.

I grind to a halt. "It's Amber!" I want to call after him, but I don't. I can't. My chest burns and my side aches. I struggle to the water station and grab two cups. I dump one on my head, chug the other, and start the trek back.

Racers of all ages and shapes catch me now, but my scrawny legs slow to a crawl. Damn Jill! If she were here, I'd have someone to trudge on with. At the very least, someone to suffer with.

I peel my phone from its encasement and fumble my slick thumbs on the screen.

You owe me Big Time.

I start to squeeze the phone back in its holder, but Lady Gaga wails. A text. Jill.

Would you want this? It reads. A picture of a vomit-filled toilet fills the screen. My feet stutter, and fruit loops climb my throat. I buckle, heaves wrenching my tender belly.

A fleshy hand strokes my back. "You okay, Sweetie?" Phyllis asks.

I ease my head from between my knees and reswallow my breakfast. Phyllis hands me a half-empty bottle of water.

"This'll help." She rubs my back. "Just sips now, you hear?"

I squeeze out a smile. "Thanks, Phyllis." I swish a mouthful. "Don't wait for me." I sway upright and swat the air with my hand. "Go on."

A smile covers Phyllis's face. She turns, and her plump frame bustles down the near-empty street. The crowd is well past us now.

My stomach still threatens to fling soggy cereal on the pavement. My feet struggle to a moseying pace.

"Last mile!" an overly cheery race official shouts. He holds up a sign. Commonwealth Power Always Finishes First.

I want to smash it over his fan-cooled head. To hell with Commonwealth Power. To hell with team leader. I narrow my eyes and glare at him. But it's not him I catch in my gaze. It's Grandma Phyllis, still tottering along.

My foot catches uneven asphalt, and I check my balance. Sweet, geriatric, and obese Phyllis is going to beat me? A renewed energy surges inside, but reality kicks in. How the hell am I going to finish this race, much less, beat Phyllis? If only I had—

I don't finish the thought. I'm too busy struggling with the hidden zipper on my pants, searching for the if-all-else-fails reserves. An inhaler and a mini-Snickers.

I take a puff, and the medicine hits me like lightning. My feet are already picking up as I scarf the Snickers.

My legs burn as hot as the sun on my forehead, but the sugar and adrenaline push me past the overweight guy who's as big as double cubicle, past Phyllis, and past the finish line.

A volunteer shouts my time, but time isn't important. I finished! I did it! I—

I'm thirsty as hell.

Out of breath, my mouth drier than burnt toast, I make my way to the water cooler. I take a cold bottle and press it to my forehead. My pulse slows, and the heat subsides from my face, but there's something else.

A shiver. It crawls up my spine, through my shoulders, and down my arms. But it's not from the cold bottle.

A few feet away, sparkling blue eyes smile at me. Not just any eyes. Dane's eyes. He grins and steps toward me, offering his towel. I take it and dab my cheeks. I'm so close I catch a whiff of his aftershave.

"Thanks." I hand it back.

He waves away his towel, his smile broadening. "You keep it."

He laughs and walks away. I can only stare, so stunned the towel slips from my grasp. I reach down and retrieve it.

"Great job, Allie," Mr. Palmer says.

I rush to stand and resist the urge to roll my eyes, but the annoyance in my voice is evident. "It's Amber."

His brow furrows, and he smacks my arm. "Right. Go get that shirt and," he gestures to my mouth, "clean yourself up. We've got a picture to take."

He walks away, and the crowd swallows him up. My hands grip the towel. Clean myself up? How rude! It's not like we're preparing for a team huddle.

But . . . wait. Does he mean I have food on my face?

My knees buckle, and I don't dare take out my phone to check. I lift Dane's towel and wipe my mouth.

Peanut remnants and melted chocolate smear the white fabric. Snickers. I drop my head, and my stomach twists.

"What's wrong now, Sugar?"

I lift my eyes. Beads of sweat stream down Phyllis's forehead. Deep pink creeps through her dark cheeks.

She squeezes my shoulder. "We did it, Amber! We finished!"

I raise up my chin, and a smile creeps to my lips. "Yeah. We did, didn't we?"

Phyllis beams her warm smile. "Shall we grab breakfast? I know a place that serves a mean biscuits and gravy."

All feelings of nausea vanish, and a pang of hunger hits my gut. "Sure, but," I tilt my head in the direction of Mr. Palmer, "what about the group shot?"

Phyllis shifts her eyes in his direction. Her smile fades into a frown, and she shakes her head. My eyes track her gaze. Mr. Palmer is handing out ball caps to our coworkers—our *team*. Dane takes one and shakes Mr. Palmer's hand. He slips on the cap. The words *Palmer's A-Team* are embroidered on the front. I cringe. If Mr. Palmer can't even remember my name, I certainly am not on his A-team.

"I just came for the run," Phyllis says. "Not to kiss Palmer's ass."

I hoot with laughter. "Who cares about the photo," I finally manage. "I'm starving."

Phyllis nods, and I loop my elbow through hers, and we start down Cary Street.

Who wants to be a team leader, anyway?

A Question of Wisdom

Gary D. Kessler

(Inspired by the biblical story of the wisdom of Solomon, previously published in *Shadow of the Blueridge*)

When I came to, Clea was there with me on the front porch of my house on the outskirts of Buena Vista, up there in the Blue Ridge Mountains, fannin' my face for all she was worth with my letter. I sat bolt upright and grabbed for the precious letter. Night had fallen in the mountains and the fire flies and crickets were puttin' on a display.

"Don't you go mussin' that letter up, Miss Clea," I said.

"Land, Dorothy, you give me a fright. I saw you from out at the walk, you on your back on the porch, your porch light shinin' on your old legs splayed out like Raggedy Ann, an' your dress up over your nevermind. I thought you'd died and gone to heaven."

"Close enough, Miss Clea," I answered, "close enough. Here, give me that letter back."

"It's not time to be worryin' 'bout no scrap of paper, Miss Dorothy Dent," Clea Stallings muttered through pursed lips. "It be dark out. The skeeters'll get you all et up. You just get on in this house and sit down over in that chair while I call an amb'lance."

"There's no need for that," I let her know in no uncertain terms. "I don't need no ambulance. I need the preacher."

"Well, I don't really think you're that far gone, woman. I think some quiet time in that chair while I see if you have the fixin's for tea, and then we'll just see about what you need."

"Oh, I don't think I need the preacher for last rites, sister. I'm just full of hallelujahs I've just gotta let out."

"Full of somethin', I agree," Clea said through clinched teeth, "but not nec'sarily shouts of joy. Anyone in your family have a stroke at your age?"

"Stop messin' with me, Miss Clea," I countered. "OK, OK, I'm sittin' in the chair. See. I've sat in the chair. Now give

116

me that letter. I haven't had a stroke; I'm just fine. It's just that letter that gave me a start. It was just a faintin' spell. They come on on their own accord for ole folk like us. Don't mean much—until it get to the point where it don't matter anymore what it means."

"But . . ." Clea started to say. However, she stopped and just threw up her hands. "Well, OK. You sit there, and I'll go check your tea supply."

"No, Clea," I said. "You sit here a spell too. I'm just so sad and happy and mad that I just need to talk to someone about it. I've kept it inside me too long. I just don't know which way to go. But seein' as how you are here, you'll do. In fact, you'll do just fine. So, sit down and let me explain."

There for a second Clea looked like she was headed in three directions at once and just didn't know which foot to put out toward where first. Then she gave a sigh and a little wave of the letter in her hand and sat down.

"It's about this letter, ain't it?" she said, as she handed the paper and envelope to me. "Postmark is Lexington. Who you know in Lexington, Virginia, would be sendin' you a letter stead of just pickin' up the phone? Lexington just be down the mountain from here."

"Yes, it is the letter, and I'll tell you 'bout it, but first we have to let out what's gone unspoken between us for the last twenty-five years."

Clea looked at me a bit perturbed. "And what's that, missy? I thought we'd pretty much talked over ever'thing either one of us had seen or done since high school."

"Not ever'thing, Clea. Not nearly ever'thing. An I think you know that."

Clea's eyes showed she still didn't understand.

But I'd finally gotten around to it, so I gritted my teeth and dove in. "Don't you remember that time your mother told you not to go around with me anymore and you ignored her and we met secretly for years—that time right after I missed all that school?"

"Oh . . . that." Clea's voice was flat, but her face had reddened.

"I had a baby, Clea. I had a baby girl. You've been a good friend to me all these years. But we've never been able to talk 'bout it. I had a baby girl, and I wasn't married or anything. There, that's said. I don't see that that hurt either one of us. Do you?"

"N-o-o," Clea answered. "But I don't see what brought this on today. Is it 'bout this letter?"

"Yes, it is, and I'll read this letter to you. But I've got to talk a bit first. It's been scary these last twenty-five years. Things have happened that I couldn't explain—and didn't want to mention at all for fear they would just fall through—but now I want to talk 'bout it. I want to talk to someone 'bout it until it either happens or doesn't happen. Oh, I'm not makin' a lick of sense, am I?"

"Not really," Clea answered. But she sat back into her chair and gave me a reassuring look. "But you just go on and let it come out your own way and in your own time, hon. I'm listenin'. Even you decide you don't want to talk about it after all, I'm still sittin' here with you."

"Thanks, Clea. You're the best. You always have been. We never talked 'bout the baby, but you always knew, didn't you? I'm sure your mother made it all very clear when she told you to stop goin' round with me."

Clea didn't deny the statement.

"But weren't you ever curious what happened to that baby?"

"Yes, course I was. But you never brought it up, so I didn't either. I was just tryin' to keep you as a friend. And that wasn't always easy to do."

"I know, Clea—and I 'preciated ever'thing you did and was for me. I was just so beside myself in those days. I was angry at everyone and ever'thing. And I'm sure the drugs were part of it."

"Yes, I thought so too," Clea answered in a quiet voice, her eyes lowered to the tattered braided rug between the two overstuffed chairs. But then she perked up and raised her eyes to mine. "But you shook that. You were a real trooper and an inspiration to the rest of us who were givin' those drugs a try. You cleaned yourself up real fast."

She'd never told me before she'd done tried the drugs too. She were tellin' me now, though—trustin' me like I was trustin' her. It helped me let it all out.

"I had help, Clea. I had a lot of expensive help from people my folks could not afford. But that was all part of the mystery."

"What mystery?"

"I guess it's time to get to that part. I've just gotta decide where to start. It's just all so strange and mixed up."

We both sat there in silence for several minutes under that nervous light in the fixture overhead I keep meanin' to fix but don't get around to.

"OK. I guess I'll start with Cindy's birth. There really isn't much worth talkin' 'bout in my life before that. I was off at my grandma's near Lexington for that near year you didn't see me. My baby girl was mighty beautiful. I wanted to keep her so bad. I bet you didn't know—no, there was no reason for any of you to have known—but I fought to keep that baby. And I would have kept her if it hadn't been for that mix-up at the hospital."

I stopped then, and I knew that Clea was bustin' to say or ask something, but I needed to get it all out, so I jumped right back in.

"There was a suspicion that the name bands on my Cindy and on another little baby girl born about the same time had gotten switched, and the other baby—there's not a doubt in my mind that it was the other baby—died before they could get that straightened out."

A sound came out of Clea, but I ignored it and forged ahead.

"Well, that other mother was older than me, and a whole lot richer than me—and she had a husband in tow and I was all by myself. She kept screamin' that Cindy was her baby and all about how she was too old to have another baby. This last part alone was enough to tell me she knew Cindy was my baby and that hers had died. But that woman had connections and money and position, and she had lawyers and a judge in that hospital so fast that I didn't even have a chance to think what I was goin' to do. Next thing I knew was that the judge in

Lexington was sayin' he couldn't sort it all out and that maybe the best thing to do was to send the baby over to Social Services there in Lexington until we could go to court. I wasn't no dummy even then, even with all those bad choices and the drugs. I could tell where this was goin' between the likes of me and the likes of that woman—and I didn't want to see my baby over in the Social Services system for the months or years it would take for this to go through the courts. Because of what my daddy did to my momma, I'd come out of that system myself. That was why I was so messed up myself."

I must have been cryin' at this point and bunchin' myself up and trying to disappear into the chair cover design, because Clea got up, came over and sat on the chair arm, encircled me with her arms, and started patting me on the back. That felt good.

"There, there, Dot. You don't have to explain or justify anything to me."

"I know that, Clea. But it's time I explained and tried to justify this to myself. I haven't really had to do that all these years. That's what's so strange. Where was I? Oh, yes, I did what was sensible and what I knowd was gonna happen anyway. I told that old judge that Cindy was my baby, there was gonna be no denying of that on my part, but that I could see I probably wasn't gonna to get her and I didn't want her goin' to Social Services, so that old Mrs. Landon could have her. The judge gave me the longest, deepest look before he—"

Clea sat bolt upright. "Mrs. Landon? Cindy. You're talkin' about Cynthia Landon. Of the Landons just up the block?"

I just nodded and continued. "That's right. My Cindy has been livin' right up the block from me for the last twenty-five years. It's been a real miracle—and a heartbreak at the same time. You know this isn't the neighborhood I came from. You was just as surprised as I was when I inherited this house with all the trimmings from somewhere mysterious right after high school—we always thought it somehow was Steve's people in remorse for him gettin' me pregnant and then just walzin' off. But as far as I know, they weren't rich people either.

"For a while I had the fantasy that Mrs. Landon was behind it, but she never showed that much care for either me or Cindy. After high school, there was the paid-up drug rehab for me and there were the job offers, first at the nursery school where Cindy attended, then in the cafeteria of Cindy's elementary and high schools, and finally in the real estate office where Cindy worked right before she got married. The biggest miracle of all was how Cindy and I became close friends and how she's spent so much time over here because Mrs. Landon has all of those garden clubs and all that charity work to attend to. When Cindy got married, I was the one who was bridal coordinator. Mrs. Landon may have been sittin' in the family pew, but I was the one who sewed Cindy into her dress and who had the last word with her before she walked down that aisle."

It was getting along toward dark now, and I found myself tunin' into the front window, lookin' out at the street light in the front of the house, wonderin' if the front gate would creak and there'd be steps on the walk—or not. What bittersweet wonderings.

Clea broke the silence. "That's quite a story, quite a story to have locked up within you all these years. Both wonderful and tragic. It's all a little much for me. But why? Why now? Why did you faint on the porch, and what does this have to do with that letter?"

I sighed. I'd gone this far with it. Clea deserved to know the rest—to know what I'd only now learned myself.

"Did you read the obituaries in the paper yesterday?" I asked her.

"Yes, of course. You know I always read the 'bituaries," Clea snorted. "How many times have you heard me say Amen because my name wasn't listed there yet?"

"Judge Alexander down in Lexington died."

"Why, yes he did. I did read that." A pause. "Judge Alexander. You don't mean he was the judge who—?"

"Yes, yes he was. He was the judge who gave my baby to Mrs. Landon. His lawyer sent over this letter to me today. A letter he said Judge Alexander gave him to give to me. The lawyer said there was a letter to take to Cindy at the same time."

There wasn't much else that needed to be done now beyond reading the letter to Clea.

"Miss Dorothy Dent," I read,

> If only we had the wisdom at the beginning of our careers that we have at the end of them, we judges would be something to behold. I am writing you this letter, one among many I have had to write from my long years on the bench, to try to clear both of our minds of one great question mark, something I seem only able to do on my deathbed. I want to confess, although I was certainly aware at the time that you were not fooled for a minute, that I knew that the baby you gave up in the hospital all those years ago was rightfully yours.
>
> I don't really know even after all these years of life and of work on the bench what the right thing to have done for that baby was. You were still a child yourself, on drugs, with no prospects for yourself, let alone for a baby. From a humanitarian standpoint, giving the baby to the Landons might have been the best for everyone involved, especially for the baby. Even you, at the time, seemed to know that it was best to give the baby up. But I do know that I didn't do my duty when I accepted your decision, knowing without a doubt, based on your willingness not to put the baby in jeopardy, that the baby really was yours. For, you see, I was paid for a favorable decision by the Landons. I took their money.
>
> I beg your forgiveness for having done that. The only thing I can offer up to mitigate my guilt is to let you know, after all these years, where that money from the Landons went. It went to put you through a good drug

rehabilitation program, so that you could be a mother to your baby if you ever regained custody; it went to that house on the same block as the Landon's and next to the playground where your baby would play. And when the money ran out, I did what I could to put you near your daughter in your jobs.

I cannot say whether I was wise or foolish to be a party in separating you from your baby in the first place. If judges learn one thing in their careers of being asked to play God, it's that they can't come anywhere close to the wisdom of God. The complex problems of real life and the competing demands for justice just do not permit simple solutions. But if I can give you any comfort in the here and now, let me tell you that your decision to give your baby a better chance at life than you had, and your determination to take every opportunity that came your way to be part of your baby's life, show that you had more wisdom than the rest of us put together in the bad choices that faced us in that hospital.

As my attorney should have told you when delivering this, I also have sent a similar letter to—

The sounds I so wanted to hear crashed through my reading of the letter. The creak of the front gate; light, but quick, insistent footsteps on the walk. My baby was home.

Hollow Night

Olivia Stowe

"More wine, Shelley?" Peter asked in a "maybe you've had enough" tone.

"Yes, please," I answered, turning my gaze back to the last of the lingering sunset behind the Allegheny Mountains on the other side of the Shenandoah Valley. I was a bit amused at what must be a conundrum for him—wondering if I'd had too much to walk a straight line but enough to make his obvious intentions easier. I had come on the date anticipating—and even welcoming at the time—his intentions. Nearness hadn't made my heart grow fonder, though.

I had already decided that I would jolly well stop well short of Peter's intentions. I mean he was good looking enough and he was talked up by Sally Ann, if not by the other women faculty members I knew. But I had found that he was too full of himself to have room for me as well. And as wildly interesting as he was, he was boring. I giggled at the thought of the contradiction, yet the "rightness" of that, which might have been a signal that I, indeed, had had quite enough wine.

Days later I wondered if it was just the wine. I certainly hope not, although details of that evening have become more hazy rather than clearer with the passage of time.

We were on the Jennings's—or was it Jenkins . . . whatever—deck, at their Wintergreen townhouse condo. Peter had brought me to the tented concert hall by the resort lodge earlier in the evening for a fall orchestra concert—an annual Halloween evening tradition. He had asked me if I wanted to stop off at his friends' mountain condo after the concert before driving back to Staunton, in the valley. Wintergreen was a ski resort community perched above the Blue Ridge Parkway and crowning the Blue Ridge Mountain range near where Interstate 64 crossed the mountains.

I'd agreed readily to put off an awkward homecoming as long as possible. I knew he'd want to come in when he returned me to my apartment, and I had already had quite enough of him. Unfortunately, he hadn't had enough of himself yet. I'd been warned about him when I'd joined the faculty of Mary Baldwin University in the English Department. He was the chair of the History Department. But of course I hadn't heeded the warning. I'd listened more to Sally Ann, who was head over heels for him. He really was quite good looking—more so with his mouth shut, though.

Happily, Stewart Jenkins—or was it Steve?—had wound Peter up by asking how the Skyline Drive, starting just north of where we were sitting and winding around on top of the Blue Ridge Mountains up to Front Royal, near the top of the valley, had come to be. The history of the Skyline Drive obviously was one of Peter's pet subjects. With a sigh, I took another swig of my wine—a very good King Family winery viognier—and wrapped my new Monet lily pond–motif scarf and silk jacket more tightly around me. Going on autopilot, I stared into the firepit and the last vestiges of a red and purple sunset beyond blue mountains off the west, while Peter waxed eloquent and oh so erudite.

"They started plans for a heaven highway—spanning the top of the world along mountain summits—accessible from Washington, D.C., as early as the mid 1920s, under Calvin Coolidge," he said. "It took them until 1934, under FDR, to clear the original landholders off over 150,000 acres of mountain-top land—which wasn't easy to do. Hidden homesteads were tucked away in the folds and hollows of the mountain, where people were living under the most primitive conditions. And these, mind you, were mostly people whose families had been there for generations, from the earliest days of the expansion west, and who had no intention of leaving at all. But the government was persistent and often brutal. By 1940 there were estimated to be fewer than a hundred mountain people hiding out in the hollows, but the last of them wasn't deemed to have been ferreted out and resettled or to have died until nearly 1980."

"Estimated," you said, our host interjected, with a question in his voice. "Are you saying there are still holdouts in the hollows of the mountains below us?"

"Who knows?" Peter said with a shrug. Then, showing a mischievous smile, he said, "It's Halloween. Maybe the spirits of the displaced families return for one night—this night—every year to haunt those who forced them out of their homes."

"Sounds like the making of a scary story," our host said, showing by the amusement in his voice that he wasn't much scared. Both men laughed.

"But seriously," Peter said, returning to his lecture mode, "the initial work, once started, only was able to go on for eight years—because World War Two came along. But by then . . ."

I lost all interest in his dissertation at that point—or rather gained interest in where he'd set the wine bottle down—and when I had refilled my glass, I sighed contentedly and got lost in the fire. I was in the mood to plunge into the flames. All keyed up and no one to help me in my need.

I tuned back in when hearing the emphasis put on "men."

"It was quite a feat, forging a road along the spine of the Blue Ridge," Peter was saying. "Roosevelt had created a men's construction work force to provide jobs in the Depression, and he set a thousand of them, the Civilian Construction Corps, to carve out the Skyline Drive."

"Men? All men?" our host asked.

"I would presume so," Peter answered. "It was backbreaking work. Some men died building the drive. Hardly work for women."

Of course, hardly not, I thought, and, controlling myself from giving a snort, returned to focusing on my wine glass and the enticement of the fire pit.

An hour later, as we were leaving, Peter, turned to me, shook his head like he was my father and catching me on a bad habit, and said, "Don't forget your scarf. You almost left it in the car. It fell on the deck when you stood." I could almost hear him say, rather, "while you were trying to stand." "And you had to go back for it after the concert too," he added, unnecessarily. I had gotten the point. I didn't usually wear a scarf and had only done so tonight because I knew it would be colder on the mountaintop than down in the valley. And the scarf was new.

"Thank you," I answered a bit icily and retrieved my Monet-patterned scarf. I dared not say more, as I felt I was slurring my words. I wondered if that was as obvious to Peter as it was to me.

We took the short rise to the top of the mountain at night from the Wintergreen entrance in Peter's beloved and much—too much—praised and described vintage BMW convertible. At the ridgeline, we crossed the Blue Ridge Parkway and then plunged down again on a steep, winding, narrow road that was to take us past Sherando Lake at the base of the mountains and hence through Waynesboro and back to Staunton. It was dark, the trees came right up to the side of the gravel, and the road forked more than once. Peter claimed to know just which forks to take—it was clear he was anxious to get back to Staunton—and, I was afraid, to my apartment. He drove too fast for the conditions, but he was a good driver.

There was nothing he could do about the clunky sound that abruptly escaped the engine compartment, though, and that prompted him to pull into an overgrown and rutted driveway to avoid someone coming upon our stopped car in the road when coming down the mountain behind us and crashing into us.

Peter exited the car, lifted the hood, poked around while I stood nearby holding a flashlight, and demonstrated that a university department head was conversant with pretty crude profanity.

"That's it, then," he said. "It can be fixed, but it will take more than one person and considerable time." He explained that someone would have to lift this and hold it out of the way without detaching its cables while he fixed something else under it, which, in itself, could take half an hour or more. He, of course, named the parts, but I, of course, didn't remember what they were. He also looked expectantly and hopefully at me, and I quickly told him, "Well, don't look at me, I'm afraid. I paid $200 for this skirt and blouse set and you're already filthy from the oil." I didn't also say that I was so shaky from the wine that I couldn't trust myself to hold an awkward piece of machinery up in the dark for upwards of an hour, while he worked under it with his precious hands. He didn't argue the point, so he probably was thinking the same.

We looked around. The mountains appeared to rise in all directions from us. We were truly back into one of the mountain hollows, where we quickly found there was no cellphone reception. Amazingly enough, we saw the glimmer of lights further down the track we'd pulled into.

"This is still part of the park," Peter said. "There shouldn't be anyone living back there."

"Should we try it, or should we try walking back up or down the road to find help?" I asked. I had purposely said "we." There was no way I was going to stay out here on the side of a dark mountain at night by myself.

"Those lights certainly are closer," Peter said.

Brilliant deduction.

We stumbled down the overgrown drive, which, like the roads before it, forked. We took the right fork because that appeared to lead to the lights. It didn't. The old wooden farmhouse, which proved to be partially lit by lantern light—was off to the left, but there was a footpath from the drive we were on over to it, and we took that.

As we came nearer, we heard the music—a man singing in a soft, melodic baritone and lightly strumming a guitar.

He didn't act surprised at all as we approached the front porch, where he was sitting on a rickety cane-seat chair and playing the guitar. He watched us approach with a slight smile and no surprise, as if he'd expected us—I'd even say a slightly dopey smile if he wasn't such a handsome and well-put-together young man. And those mesmerizing pale-blue eyes. He was wearing bib coveralls, but, as far as I could see, nothing else. He was barefoot. This last day of October was unseasonably warm—but not *that* warm, I wouldn't think. I'll have to admit—we can blame it on the wine and my irritation that Peter hadn't proved to be a divine date—that the young man had a sensual effect on me.

Although it appeared to be no surprise in him that we had popped up, he did stop singing and strumming, looked at us briefly in silence without losing his somewhat sloppy smile, and, while still capturing me with his eyes, made me jump by calling out, "Pa. Ma. Tommy. Jack. We got visitors."

Peter and I were standing at the base of the wooden steps up to the porch when the summoned family came to the front door, barred only by a slitted screen door, and peered out at us. They looked like they had just walked off the set of a program about the Waltons' poorer relatives. Three men, one older and two young and strapping like the young man sitting and singing on the porch—all in greasy bib overalls. And, teetering beyond them, with them towering over her, a mousy looking, skinny woman in a tired cotton shift covered by a soiled frilly bib apron.

Was that blood dribbling down her apron front, I wondered. Or was I on edge because of Halloween and Peter's scary story?

Despite being shielded behind the men and looking sickly against their robust physiques, the woman quickly proved to be in charge.

"And who might you be? I'm busy canning tomatoes," she said in a tired, slightly put-upon voice.

Of course, if we'd known you were canning tomatoes, lady, I thought, we wouldn't have decided to throw a rod through our car engine in your driveway. I didn't say that out loud, though. These looked like people who would shoot you with a shotgun as soon as spit in your eye.

But then the woman checked herself and smiled wanly. "But that's no way to greet visitors. What can we do for you? You must be in a spot of trouble to be visiting this late of night in the mountains."

Peter told them what the problem was, and, to their credit, under the woman's direction, the three men standing at the door mobilized themselves to go off with him immediately to aid us in our distress. "You stay here, Billy Ray," the woman said to the younger man sitting on the porch—who hadn't budged from his chair. "You'd just be in the way anyway."

As the three men clattered down from the porch and past me, picking up Peter along the way, the woman said, "Billy Ray'll give you no problem, Miss. He's just a little slow."

Within seconds it was just me standing before the porch stairs, Billy Ray sitting in his chair and giving me a somewhat silly, but melting smile, and Ma in the door. Seconds later, with a "You can come in or stay out here as you like, but I have to get back to my canning," the woman had turned and left. I climbed the stairs to the porch, smiling at Billy Ray as I moved, and he smiled back. I was lost in those pale-blue eyes. At the door, I looked into the stark, worn-wood interior of the house. All I could see from here was a living room and dining room, sparsely furnished with crude, worn-out, mismatched furniture. The lantern light came from the kitchen beyond.

I was about to enter the house when I saw it—the carcass of a deer hanging from the ceiling in the dining room. No matter where I sat or stood in the living or dining rooms, I would be facing a dead deer carcass. I turned back and moved to an old rocking chair on the porch on the other side of the front door from where Billy Ray had returned to strumming his guitar and singing an achingly beautiful song in his soft, low baritone. As he sang, he watched me.

It wasn't just his singing that was achingly beautiful. So was he. Young, obviously muscular as his bib overalls didn't effectively cover much. Blue eyed, but black haired, with a lock hanging down into his face, giving me the urge to go over to him and brush it out of his eyes.

He was singing a love song. I realized that the lyrics were quite suggestive. It was more than a love song. I blushed, but I continued to listen, straining to catch the lyrics

He stopped singing and we sat there, still maintaining eye contact, both of us swaying a bit in our chairs.

"Here, come over here, Little Darlin'," he whispered to me, extending an arm toward me. "I know what you came here for."

How could he know when I didn't know myself? Nevertheless, I rose and walked over to him—very close to him. I have no idea why I did that. He would think I was easy—I *was* being easy. Maybe it was the wine; maybe it was because I had expected something with Peter and now didn't want that with Peter. It doesn't matter what I thought. I went to him.

He put his cheek on my belly and I brushed the lock of hair out of his eyes with my hand. One of his hands went to and under the hem of my skirt and worked its way up, up above my knee. I leaned my face down, breathing in the unexpectedly clean, smoky smell of his hair, and applied my lips to the top of his head.

* * * *

"I would walk you to your door, but . . ."

"Certainly you mustn't," I said, opening the passenger door of the BMW convertible and putting one foot out onto the pavement. This part was working out quite well. "You need to go straight home and see if you can salvage any of your clothes. Despite the little mishap, it was a fine evening, Peter. Thank you."

Between them, Peter and the mountain men had gotten the BMW going again, but not without getting Peter covered with auto grease and oil. Papa and his boys probably were too, but it was harder to tell if their overalls were in worse condition now than before Peter and I had descended on them. In any case, I had avoided any fumbling at my apartment door, and Peter certainly wouldn't be forward enough to ask to come in to take a bath in my tub.

"Pedro doesn't usually act up like this," Peter said.

"Pedro?"

"The car." Peter lovingly patted the dashboard behind the steering wheel.

Of course. Peter had named his car. And more of course—he'd named it after himself.

"Tomorrow. At the university?"

"It's Saturday already. I don't have any classes today," I answered.

"Pity, I do."

Yippee, I thought. A day will naturally be put between now and the future with Peter.

"When you do return to work . . . you won't . . ."

"I won't mention the mishap," I said. "I'll only say how divine going to a concert up at Wintergreen and watching the sun set behind the Alleghenies was." I tactfully didn't include having spent the time with him.

"Splendid," he said. I don't know if he didn't want me to say his beloved BMW had broken down in the mountains and we were thrown on the mercy of hillbillies in the hollows or if he didn't want me to reveal that he hadn't had his way with me. Either way, he could bet I wouldn't be talking much about this date—especially the part about how much I'd forgotten myself up at the farmhouse in the hollow and how sluttish I'd been. Not that I had any regrets about that.

I was fully sober now, and I wasn't completely clear about the particulars of the night, but I had no trouble remembering the essentials.

After I'd waved and smiled encouragingly to Peter and turned to walk up the series of brick steps to the entrance to my apartment house, I let my mind go to tomorrow and not having to go to work. I knew exactly what I'd be doing tomorrow. As well as helping Peter get the BMW working again, the mountain men had given him detailed directions on getting out of the hollow we'd trapped ourselves in by a series of misguided turns. Peter had had no trouble following the directions. For my part, I had carefully mapped the turns out in my mind as well.

* * * *

Looking for—and then finding—the farmhouse deep in the hollow of the Blue Ridge Mountains, above Sherando Lake, in the daylight and sober, wasn't anything like I remembered it at night half looped and more than half out of control. When I was there—if "there" was the house I'd been looking for— some things about the walk into the farmhouse from the road and about the old farmhouse once I'd gotten to it seemed familiar. But in greater part, something was "off" and not as I thought it would be. The grounds were more overgrown, the walk from the road was both longer and not in quite the same direction as I remembered it. There was little evidence that a car had broken down at the entrance to the drive toward the house. Peter had come away with more grease and oil on him

132

than I could see evidence of on the ground where I was sure the car had died.

The house I found seemed more derelict than the one from the previous night. The wood was more worn. More was broken or missing. The house leaned. Surely the house from the previous night didn't lean toward the east as this one did. Most different—and disappointing—was that this house had obviously been abandoned, and abandoned some decades earlier. Last night there had been a family here. There had been lantern light. There had been a father and two sons helping Peter get his car going again. There had been a weary mother canning tomatoes.

There had been a disarming and compelling young man sitting on the porch, rocking, and singing seductive songs in a sweet, low baritone.

Today this house was empty—long abandoned, long unkept and long unloved.

I gingerly climbed up to the porch, afraid I would go through the rotting floorboards with each step. There were two straw-seated chairs, one on each side of the door, just as the previous night. But neither of them looked like they would support the weight of a child, let alone me . . . or Billy Ray. I remembered his name today. Last night, as Peter drove me home, I found I'd forgotten it—and not being able to surface it had driven me mad. What was real and what wasn't? Today I knew his name was Billy Ray. That seemed so real. But there was no evidence of him or his guitar on the porch now, in the light of day.

The screen door screening was shredded, just like the previous night. The interior I could see from the door was as bleak as it had been in the night. Even then it had had an abandoned look. I looked into the dining room, beyond the living room, building up the courage to do so. No deer carcass. There was a hook in the ceiling there, but there wasn't any blood on the floor under it. Had there been a pan under the hanging carcass last night? I couldn't remember. Had there even been a hanging deer carcass? Who hangs the carcass of a deer in their dining room? What was real? What wasn't?

There certainly was at least one thing real about last night, I thought, blushing at the thought of it.

I entered the house and moved to the kitchen, beyond the dining room. The woman had been canning tomatoes, she'd said. There certainly should be evidence of that in the kitchen. There wasn't. There wasn't even any evidence that canning could be done in there. There was an old hand-crank water pump over the sink. I went over and cranked it. A thin stream of water resulted. At least that worked. Sort of.

I stood, leaning against the sink, breathing heavily and trying to reason it out in my mind. Was there another house out here I'd missed—a near duplicate? There had been one drive in from the road, which split. It was possible—even likely—that two houses had been built back here on the same plan at one time and that I'd found the wrong one today.

But would the outbuildings added over time be the same? There was one that was vivid in my mind.

I turned and hurried through the house, out to the porch, and down into the yard. There, instinctively, I turned to the right and strode down a path to a shed off to the side. I stopped and regulated my breath and willed my heart to stop thumping at the door before pushing the door open and entering the small space.

It was what I expected—what I remembered—but, once again, more deteriorated and dusty and with a greater a sense of abandonment than the previous night. Still, the double bed was there and the old, yellowed mattress. But there was no bedding. I couldn't be sure. And I'd been buzzed on wine last night—and off my guard. Most important, there was no one here. I wouldn't have come up here at all today if I hadn't thought he'd be here.

But he obviously wasn't here. Maybe I'd never been here either.

I was about to leave when I saw it, draped over a straight chair, picked out by a beam of light from an open window.

A scarf. A Monet lily pond–patterned scarf. The scarf I kept losing.

POETRY

Chasing

Stanley A. Galloway

IAD-DEN

Rising through the clouds that have witnessed sunset,
time turns back,
as if Isaiah's hand were raised,
and slowly the sun rises in the west
to hover just above a pierced horizon.
We chase the sun as only Marvell's gods can do
see the orange turn apricot then butternut
each variation on display for slow evaluation
lingering, tempting one to wander in unnatural time.

Would that first we were together
and had put aside all coyness
allowing for two hundred years of time perceived
and then were locked in full embrace
throughout this supernatural stretch of day.
Would that space were also stopped
and that place beyond the night's horizon
and the place where I now sit
were one
with you.

This is no supernatural stay for military need
but opportunity to multiply the witness of our adoration
chasing the pink penumbra at the world's edge.
At last the sun looks jealously on my desire—
Lady, were you here, how we could make him run.

Winter, 1820

Stanley A. Galloway

Sometimes I am Keats, sometimes Fanny Brawne
one leaving, one left behind
acknowledged thorn, a spot of blood
raging at the sun, seeing no beauty in its red
confined in bandages of Italy or chilly England

Called away against my will, too weak
to march against the battery
where my elastic spirit stretches thin in wonder
if our three bright days of summer butterflies are set or if
my hope in temporary cloud might prove improbably correct

This posthumous existence requires
a blacker word than *black* to match
the void I find here every day without a letter
no necrophilic kiss from brain to heart reanimating words
no comfort in a hurtling Roman moon.

Proteus' Lament

Stanley A. Galloway

*for you are over boots in love, | And yet you never swum the Hellespont.**

If I could swim the Hellespont I would
but continents of land resist the lover's
stroke, and I hold dust and gravel in
the place of night's warm post-wave clasp. The point
of hell, instead, mocks shape's security.

The cava drained and slept away—clear-eyed
you, blinking at a startling sun, depart.
You leave a measured-and-found-wanting heart.

If I but sought for honor, not for love,
some measure of success I might hold here
but we have wrestled past and extant dogs
survived the bone-deep pain—yet come unglued.
I shrink: no moon, no after-swim embrace,
one sharp translucent heart-sore sigh,
the right of recklessness, wit's wearied loss.

* Valentine to Proteus in *Two Gentlemen of Verona* 1.1.25-26,
William Shakespeare

Holiday Rain, with Solo Oboe

Stanley A. Galloway

a hundred hours
a hundred days
a hundred years, I've been
caught in neverendin' jingle-beltin' rainfall
wishin' it were stars and snowflakes
fallin' on the pavement of my numb Virginia soul
or April fog wisp-shimmyin' beside the Seine
miles away on fuzzy streetlit banks:
no, I've got no weather but his rain—
no eggnog noggin' on me
red-eyed from an empty sleigh
ev'ry chestnut sizzlin' on someone else's fire
leavin' Parson Brown without a reason
to be waitin' in the cold:
no, I've got no carol—
just this bone-damp holiday bombardment
pitti-pitti-patterin' inside
ever since your last good-bye
when you said I'd never
never change
my two-tongued heart

Night Game on Long Mountain

David Black

(First place poetry, *Skyline* contest, 2017)

Say, then, that you want the world to be smaller.
There's too much of this mountain,
too many heights and crevasses and mysteries.
Say you want things known and intimate,
boundaries to be closer and friendlier
than the shadows now heavy under the pines.
Say you want life to be comfortable and visible,
like your cabin and bed.

Say you go in and build a fire,
push the dark back to the windows,
and lie in the tightness of your bunk.
Assume the hickory logs will last all night;
believe hard as you can that if you stare
at the fire long enough, sleep will comfort you.

From somewhere behind the cabin walls,
hear the sounds of eyelids closing.

Winter Morning, -13

David Black

Waking up in longjohns and socks
under so many quilts your body hurts,
windows rattling in the winds
and puffs of snow sprinkling
the sill and the floor beneath—

you fire up the stove with dry cobs and oak,
lean into it and rub your hands,

your mind unsettled by the linoleum rug,
which won't lie still. When a squall hits broadside,
the rug rises, billows. You press a foot and pump it slowly,

feel it push back against your toes
too soft for something that cold,
spongy as moss beside a spring.

Pants and shirt now, then ham and red-eye gravy,
eggs, yesterday's biscuits,
coffee as hot as you can take it
while three feet away snow won't melt.

Last fall's venison in the freezer is warmer than this,
but you're not that dead, not yet. There are chores out there,

and at the mill logs whose frozen hearts
will make a four-foot blade cut a crooked track.

Into as many layers as will fit.
Wrap a towel around your head,
another around your neck,
walk to the door. Beneath your feet
you feel the rug rippling
and you think of summer

and a field of clover
rising and falling, rising and falling,
and how every green and growing thing will die.

Country Neighbors

David Black

The new plantings were milkweed, lavender,
and butterfly weed—bait for my own eyes
and that was reason enough—but alluring, too,
to *Lepidoptera* and *Apis* and all manner
of Latinate neighbors whom I hoped to entice
into front-porch visits: **Oh, there you are!**
Come in! Sit a spell. Have a cookie and some
        sweet tea.

And they came, by the dozens, the hundreds,
lighting and leaving in haste
or sitting for a second helping,
and those greedy bumblebees—
habitués who seemed never to leave—
hefty enough to sway lavender stems
almost to the ground,
something there that kept them busy until nightfall.

And then the faithful old-timers: shy fawns and rabbits,
crazy bluejays, and the erratic swoop
of pileated woodpeckers scalloping the air
beneath their wings . . .
all these taking some from spring's first platter,
more from summer's plenty, and a few stragglers
from the last pickings of fall,

and I—I harvesting all I can as I write,
but leaving this rich world still filled
with trees and flowers and birds,
bumblebees and butterflies,
from which my poem takes only a few.

The Drunk in the Middle of the Night

David Black

That late-night insomnia once more, and
I mix my one bourbon-and-ginger ale,
pick up pen and notebook again and try
another opening line, distracted
by the smell of the whiskey, recalling
for just one short moment the rare few times
of excess in my needy college years.

Then a thought I had not had in decades—
back to one of those odd moments that came
with rural life in older days, up late
with book or TV and then came a knock
on the door, a slurred call, "Anyone here?"
and I knew it was some wandering drunk
on my back road, looking for a ride home.

I'd get him in the VW, trusting
he would recall a route number, landmark,
neighbor's name—something to help me get him there.
As the car filled with BO and whiskey fumes,
we drove in some approximate direction
long enough for a thought to click, some tree
or silo to tell him he was close to home.

Likely you won't have this three a.m.
encounter with a stranger, no story
of meandering through the county
to alarm the family with the next day.
Long before he ever reaches your farm,
he'll push a button on his phone, and at home
someone he knows answers and comes looking.

There's some loss there I regret, something gone
that speaks well of random things, of an hour
that could have become three, on a dirt road

that I was told went by Crowell's red barn
which I was told I could not fail to see
even in the pitch dark at three a.m.
since it had to be just where he knew it was.

The Woodbugger

David Black

Archaic names go from *bug* to *bogey*,
bugbear, *bogeyman*, and on to *bugger*,
even the more sonorous *bugaboo*.

It was *boogeyman* when my parents scared
me with stories of the punishing brute
who'd steal me away if I misbehaved—
stories long dead only to be revived
when my son pointed to a beer bottle
and said, "It's local and it's pretty good."

It was named "Woodbugger," and the label
displayed a cartoonish hairy creature—
our Bigfoot, the yeti of our own hills
and swamps—a name I'd never heard before,
but a beast I think I would like to meet.

I've walked my own woodland many a time
and found turtle shells, antlers, bobcat spoor—
but no huge footprint to cast, no thigh bone
above my mantel to say "He was here."
Still, I hope some day to produce a hair,
that photo, the musky carcass that says
we've lived with these shy creatures for years.

And I suggest he's a noble being,
surely deserving of a better name—
something Latinate, I think, elegant
and unpronounceable, a tag worthy
of a tall, chary visitor who lurks
behind my japonica bush and haunts
my dreams at night.

Call of the North

Jack Trammell

(A series of poems in the tradition of the Yukon)

Exclamation of the North

Sunlight draws long strokes of distance
Touching mountain talus slopes that chase gravity.

Filled with man-made curiosity I look around at
Flying pyramids made of carbon and ice . . .

Was this the (rock) face that launched a thousand ships, or
Insane greed for adventure that was named Klondike?

Cold comes in many forms and many temperatures, though
Lack of imagination must be the coldest of all.

Still, men and women come here now and
Make mockery of wilderness obstacles,

I am here against the will of the cold
And seeking something only the bards understand.

Eureka

(Inspired by an adventure and conversation along Dawson's
Creek with Audrie; edited by Randy Salzman and Audrie
Trammell)

>Many a man has staked a claim
>>Along the Bering Creek,
>Many a man has frozen there
>>With winter at her peak . . .

But Frank McClean, an ivied dean

Defied the Yukon gods,
Frank McClean loved words yet dreamed
    Of brutal conflict against the odds

Each night he read word for word
    The masters affectionately,
He longed to be, a god-like he
    In a Shakespearean tragedy

In Alaska's soil, he spent his soul
    Within a deepening pit,
And out came rock and dirt and scree
    Phantoms from Sheol

He mucked and slaved, cried and moaned
    He forgot all reading time,
He dug and scrapped to find the seam
    Sold his horses for that mine

Til, past midnight in one dark and dreary light
    He scratched a splendid gleam,
Breathless and near delirious
    He beheld the prospector's dream . . .

A nugget bold, and Oh, so great
    It sparkled, jewel of fate,
Just a bit exposed enough to see
    Patience must dictate!

He scrapped, and picked, the clouds a mask
    The nugget grew and grew,
Frank McClean forgot life's tasks
    As he shoveled the evening through

But celebration was forced to wait
    When the sky abruptly darkened,
A storm, a storm! Of all the times
    His ramshackle cabin harkened

Snow swirled and squalled and vision vanished
  The greed he felt reverted,
He knew that warmth was needed soon
  Or his life would be averted

The mercury fell too far to tell
  It died at minus fifty,
McClean's hands were numb, his feet were dumb
  A blaze he needed swiftly

In his haste, he could not waste
  The time to gather firewood,
He fumbled about and moaned a shout
  "This nugget does me no $%#% good!"

He needed fuel to light a fire
  And something very quick,
He had to burn a thankful pyre
  But he had not a single stick

He eyes spun space to space with fear
  He scanned the room in haste,
Something here something to burn
  Before it all was waste!

His mind did make its panicked race
  Until his brain turned deathly sick,
ON the shelf, the last unchecked space
  There his books to choose and pick

The first to go was Service, Oh!
  The pain he knew was real,
Then Jack London went 'til that fuel was spent
  Yet still was little heat to feel.

Thucydides, Euripides
  He even threw in some Twain,
The classics soon were all ablaze,
  With each bright flame he cried in shame

Eventually the mercury
     Came back to colored form,
Eventually some light appeared
     And the sky was free of storm

His hands were red his feet were stings
     McClean battled back a tear
His books were gone with nights so long
     absolutely nothing left to revere

Though his nugget gold in Skagway sold
     And much coinage he had in hand,
In his heart, there was no spark
     His scholarly life now seemed damned

Many a man has staked a claim
     Along the Bering Creek,
Many a man has frozen there
     With winter at her peak

But Dean Frank McClean, his nugget gleamed
     And brought him immortal fame,
Because he spent it all on yet a different haul
     And built a library in his name

Alaskans each night now can read
     The lines that masters wrote,
Thanks to Dean Frank McClean who longed to be
     A daredevil of great note

Perspective

Bridges the gap between the mountain
    And my mind's eye;
The glacier stares down sanguine
    Until a piece falls off,
Long tumbling and agonizing moments
    Then splash into icy sound.

No man has a right to witness the earth
    Without her veil on,
Yet here she is, lace and all, shaking
    Alive and filled with the power
A newly discovering woman.

My perspective; limited by my imagination:
    Two eyes that partially see,
    Two hands that sometimes touch,
    Two ears that catch an occasional whisper,

Perspective tolerates small moments, for me,
    Wind blowing a single fireweed flower.

The Photo

Wave of memory washes briefly upon the shore;
    Pioneers, prospectors, petticoats . . .
Cold waters of the Yukon sting to the touch;
    Washed stones coalesce into people I know.

Many are the plans, but God prevails.

To hear the next swirling current murmur
    Is to hear the divine whisper . . .
Each imperfect memory brought into a face
    Or a foaming completion of a dream long gone.

Many are the plans.

A mountain peers out of the snowy mist;
    Smiles, shouts, steam whistles . . .
God prevails because people cannot;
    Old photo curls in my hand.

Give Me Once More, My Southland

Elizabeth Doyle Solomon

Give me once more, days in my Southland
where winter comes, but does not dwell—
where hibiscus blooms all the year long,
wagons have ripe tomatoes to sell.

Give me once more, live-oaks draped with moss,
Ole Man River passing New Orleans—
cargo ships carrying coal or grain,
boy fishing from the bank in faded jeans.

Give me once more, words drawling out slow,
pure chicory-coffee in the pot—
the taste of oyster-crabmeat gumbo:
these are the things that I miss a lot.

Give me once more, fam'ly gatherings,
the kind we had when Gram was alive—
this is the life I miss and I love,
sunshiny southland where good things thrive.

Mountain Storm

Elizabeth Doyle Solomon

Thunder growls, grizzly reminder
in these mountains that Storm is king:
lightning flashes over peaks where
black bears and bobcats make their dens.

Even as we watch, midnight's arms
embrace the rain which runs down slopes,
soaks our Bethel land watered by
so many springs we have lost count.

Rain drums a dance on seam-tinned roof,
this two-hundred year old cabin
watching as the centuries change,
mutely memorizing seasons.

In the eerie post-storm silence,
bobcat's cry mimics a woman's—
and a great-horned owl questions,
"Who, who-who, is this in my woods?"

Katy-dids resume their strumming,
symphony of violin-wings,
Midnight's storm has cooled these mountains,
exhaling breaths of windy sighs.

Shenandoah Mountains Easter

Elizabeth Doyle Solomon

Upon this vale of violets
I step with trepid feet—
Shenandoah's benevolence,
Creator's masterpiece.

This kaleidoscope of colors
surrounds us as we kiss—
here in this peaceful paradise
nothing can seem amiss—

not the madness of Syria,
not our Idiot-Chief—
not all the starving refugees,
nor North Korean thief.

We need no church nor vested priest,
just quiet, blesséd woods—
which once provided mountain folk
with necessary goods.

Twenty-three kinds of wildflowers,
trail of tranquility—
God has given this afternoon
to my husband and me.

Strong Words for Harsh Times

Elizabeth Doyle Solomon

She stayed up half the night
trying to save the world—
honeybees, butterflies,
the words her pen unfurled—

monuments, public lands,
each threatened to be fracked—
drilling the Arctic Sea,
polar bears, whales attacked.

Inside her gray cottage
letters piled by the door—
each one written by hand:
"Please explain, I implore."

Husband stayed up late too,
convinced our Chief's corrupt—
typed letters with harsh words:
some called him too abrupt.

Dangerous times require
fires in hearts of men—
harsh, imperative words
from typewriter or pen.

Round this world all God made,
threatened by extinction—
calls for prayer warriors,
words of strong distinction.

Dominion's Planned Destruction

Elizabeth Doyle Solomon

What's to love about a pipeline
that shears Virginia's mountaintops?
Pipelines that ultimately leak,
pollute our green lands and trout streams?

Doesn't Dominion know at all
that fracking the earth for oil
destroys forests, promotes earthquakes,
and increases global warming?

When will Dominion read the science?
they're too busy filling deep pockets,
declaring Eminent Domain
on private lands of farming folks!

Variations on the Annual Theme

Erin Newton Wells

(First place poetry, Blue Ridge Writers Chapter contest, VWC, 2017)

> *— more like air in all respects, but far*
> *more subtile.*   ISAAC NEWTON

You can see why in earlier times the air
was called aether, a liquid, how light
and sound are waves that need to be held,
that cannot lie alone in empty space.
From the mouth, sound widens in rings
to the shell of the ear on its shore,
and it gathers them in. You call,
daughter a thousand miles from here,
your voice awash in a tide of wishes,
This instrument, this slender phone,
this ship bears them to me. My day star
rises on another year, and you start
the next round of the song. *Happy*, four
of them, and one *Many more*, stretched
as long as breath will go. *I'm glad*
you were born, you always say. I, too,
am glad. Where would you be.

I know you know what hides in the word
and still say it, how *hap* bears the cargo
of its earlier age, how luck curls
at the heart of birth stars, and oceans
deliver chance. *I was just thinking of you*,
I say, but cannot bring myself to add
what I saw in the news, girls traded
and sold, found in the hold of a freighter.
They cry for their mothers. They wrap
themselves in blankets in the port,
shield their eyes from light, and their ears

from sound. None of them more
than thirteen, and lost. We outdo ourselves
to end the song with our own version.
Love/ Love you more, we always say,
rings intersecting, cutting wide arcs
in the air, being held.

Night Tune

Erin Newton Wells

(Second place poetry, *Skyline* contest, 2017)

the problem of inferring the nature of the universe
from the observed characteristics of the sample. . . .
— Edwin Hubble

The myrtle's noise of magenta crowds the space
of your absence. Its cloyed scent populates the night.
The room begins its own world with ambient heat.
Sheets are thrown aside. You remain beside me
as hollows of air, shoulder and curve of your head
impressed on the pillow where you left them
this week, and for another week. In that other place
of mountain pine and rock, astringent and dry,
you start the work away from this low, soft soil,
its percussion of growth. You need altitude,
clarity, windless and deep, visible light splattered
too near to be of use. May dark clouds not move
their whale shapes on the sky to blot the high,
weird songs sung farther from you. May you catch
faint swirls and blurs on film plate, white reversed
to black, and black to thin gray, galaxies in smears
a thumb might make on glass when holding it.
May you come back. Heat lures another, a body
barely seen in the night, black on black, no light
to limb the edge or give a glint of silver to the harp
at the mouth. Breath blows in its climb to a peak,
then down, a song pulled through a hole in the sky
and known by whales, their nocturne.

My Face an Elegy

Erin Newton Wells

(First Prize, Poetry, University/Adult, The Writer's Eye, 2016, based on *Sayed, Our House is on Fire* series, Shirin Neshat, digital pigment print; image available at http://bombmagazine.org/article/10010/shirin-neshat-s-i-our-house-is-on-fire-i; first appeared in *Writer's Eye*)

I do not know where I am. My face is my house
and wilderness now. I do not know this dry land.

Rain does not fall. Rivers do not flow. Air burns.
My thirst becomes a region. It is my sky, land.

Lines of my face are riverbeds. Where is water
for a field, I ask. What grows here on my land.

No spring comes. The almond tree sends roots
into the earth's hot center, and they die, land.

My house is on fire. The windows are in flame,
a furious plume of brightness in my eyes, land.

Pomegranates of my lips do not blossom now
or swell with seed. Now they only cry, land.

Children gathered my apricot cheeks. My eyes
were almonds to them. Everything dies, land.

My forehead was an orchard. No voices sing.
No children walk beneath trees. They fly, land.

Their arms are burned wings lifted on my roof,
my brow. Who knows how far they rise, land.

Sayed, all around you is black and empty space,
country of no welcome and no song, a dry land.

(The ghazal comes from Arabic and Persian as a poetic song of love, loss, and lament. Repetitive end words reinforce a sense of lamentation. It is used here because the art on which the poem is based is an Egyptian portrait, post-Arab Spring and the 2011 revolution, by an Iranian artist exiled from her land since the 1978 revolution.)

Not Only Charleston

(First prize, Judah, Sarah, Grace, and Tom Memorial, Poetry
Society of Virginia, 2016; first appeared in *Poetry Virginia Review
2016*)

for victims of racial hatred

You could see them over the city for a day
at least, singly or together, like sun dogs,
shiny reflection, something on the lens,
floaters in a corner of sight. They bore
their glory up. It was reassuring.

It was a way to keep them as they raised
their ebenezers, as scales fell from eyes
in silvery glitter over the city, until they
began to drift apart, dissipate and go
where the wind will take them.

We wanted to save the bright dust, catch
it from the air for the back roads where
prayer is chained and breaks apart, left
for crows, hard to see it as the same
as what hovered on the city.

Less than a dozen rose over roofs, domes,
streets, palmetto trees, the place we like
to call a holy city. And all we could do
was watch them, our faces turned
to the blue redeeming sky.

Only one rose over a dirt road and caught
in loblolly pines, where no one noticed.
We wanted to sprinkle glory there like
infection, like vaccine over Jericho,
Damascus, Emmaus, Jasper.

(January 9,1998, Jasper, Texas: James Byrd, Jr., forty-nine, was chained behind a truck, dragged for over a mile by three young men. Byrd is believed to have been conscious until his body hit a culvert and was torn apart. It was called lynching by dragging. Byrd was black, the others were white, and race was the only motivation for the crime.)

The Hunter

Erin Newton Wells

(First prize, Elizabeth Neuwirth Memorial, Poetry Society of
Virginia, 2016; first appeared in *Poetry Virginia Review 2016*)

*Andrew Wyeth, tempera, 1943, Toledo Museum of Art,
Ohio. Unusual perspective is characteristic of Wyeth.*

> Look up. If only you would look above
> > your head and past a bright red hat you wear.
> Look up, beyond the charcoal gun across
> > your arm, the barrel safely angled down.
>
> Your coat is filled with shot. Your hand is poised,
> > your fingers tense. You train for this, a twitch
> that flushes out the autumn birds, then you
> > become all steel, an oiled machine. Your eye
>
> is on the covey. When it flies, the field
> > is feathered with a blur you aim against,
> the cooling sky, the lumpy patch of hay.
> > And you become the quarry now. From here
>
> you look so small, your hat a dot of red,
> > the gun a whittled stick. Your legs draw lines
> in drying grass between the shadowed lines
> > of tree. If only you could see this field
>
> in raw and yellowed umber, the color
> > of the Brandywine, waters to your knee.
> The sycamore is monstrous overhead.
> > The arms are wide. The scaling skin is dark
>
> against the whitened bone, the leather leaves
> > alive. And yet you will not look, you will
> not see the one so absolutely still,
> > his breath held in, and you within his eyes.

They hunt you down, the field of tablet size,
        the pencil longer than your gun, and you
the needed accent with your hat, your form
        the needed focal point, the view birds see.

A Glory Around You

Erin Newton Wells

(First prize, Raymond Levi Haislip Memorial, Poetry Society of
Virginia, 2016; first appeared in *Poetry Virginia Review 2016*)

Gamma knife surgery. For Vicky

> Think of it as a universe, that dome
> at your head, like the celestial spheres
> ancients thought surrounded us. Alone
> at center the hot star moves too near
> in your world. Its music is all wrong
> for you. In the perfect beauty of your
> cerebellum it gives such adverse song,
> not as the morning stars together, pure
> and holy, but harsh, strident, and loud.
> Think of this as a glory around you,
> a saint's cap, nimbus, a miracle cloud.
> Its rays stream inward like prayer, true
> and to its mark, until the star is stunned
> with blessing, cast out by benediction.

My Grandmother's Bowl and Pitcher

Erin Newton Wells

(First prize, Loretta Dunn Hall Memorial, Poetry Society of
Virginia, 2016; first appeared in *Poetry Virginia Review 2016*)

A window. Beside it a china basin, lazy scalloped edge.
The pitcher is a soaring handle, a pouting lip, ivory.
        Light ambles in, leans on it and tells

A chip where three lines meet, the glaze gone, is a gray
shallow wedge, too small for a finger to fit.
        Here is the woman who made it.

She lifts the arch of the handle and tilts the slim throat,
the braided voice of water. Her face moves with the slip
        and slap in the bowl. A cool hello.

Both hands dip and greet her skin. Her shift is wet,
stained at the breast. Her eyes close then open
        into lakes of ease.

The horse is watching in the yard, waiting, head lifted,
nostrils tasting, the soaring curve of its back
        not filled. *Come and fly.*

It nods. Up, down. It stamps and snorts. She startles
in the open window, clanging pitcher on bowl
        at the impatient roan, her favorite.

Come and fly. The chip. The crack. She will mend it.
She dresses and goes, the two of them as one blur
        flying into my future.

Challenge

Lauvonda Lynn Young

(First place poetry, Appalachian Writers Guild, VWC, 2017)

There are so many little dyings, it doesn't matter, which of them is death.
Kenneth Patchen, poet and novelist

A writing challenge to compose a poem,
by invading the skin, of a famous person,
was intriguing, so I jumped in, carpe diem,
told my brain to run, explore, have fun.

I chose Harriet Tubman, for my quest
hoped she would not resist, the intrusion.
I even imaged, Harriet loving a guest,
although, probably, I was being delusional.

Invading Harriet's skin, proved, an order tall,
as at onset, I sickened at the sight of scars, vile
placed by a slave owner's wife, with heart, small,
who with whip in her hand, had a Devil's smile.

Worse I felt, when I moved to brain mass,
how inadequate, definitely did I feel,
as I recalled, all successes of Harriet's past,
she did so much good, it is unreal

I tried to visualize, Harriet sleeping in a swamp,
with slaves, she was helping, escape to freedom,
via the Underground Railroad, in black damp,
they laid, until morning light, did come.

Harriet, also known as "Moses," gave to humanity,
so much more: train conductor, Civil War soldier, spy,
nurse, lead the Combahee River Raid, commanding
300 free African soldiers, freedom. all, Harriet did cry.

I began to perspire, felt I might smother,
compared with Harriet, I am so inferior.
All her life, she committed to helping others,
yet, she had not one minute, of feeling superior.

After a while, my heart began to thunder
Like a bullet, I darted, out of Harriet's skin,
dragged morbid history, while weighted under,
with thoughts, of the atrocities of human sins.

Note: Credit to the World Wide Web for confirmation of
historical facts included in "Challenge."

Sister Florence Myrtle Barron

Joy Merritt Krystosek

(Second place poetry, Blue Ridge Writers Chapter
contest, VWC, 2017)

I draw her memory to me
Envision her essence   close my eyes
Garden roses and lavender emit a faint
Fragrance at the far end of the parlor
Where her casket is tucked into a columned niche
A prudent design by the builder who knows
Just how things are done by country folk
A space where a family can
View their loved one
Send them to their heavenly home
She's in a better place
I stare at her from a distance
Move closer and closer to the casket
Does someone lift me up   or do I climb to peek
Touch her alabaster skin   hard and smooth
A death mask of pale, polished stone
Doesn't she look good
She's in her Sunday best
Her purple flowered dress
Baptist women don't usually wear bright colors
Jesus-on-the-Cross chain around her neck
A hint of rouge on her cheeks and lips
Baptist women don't usually wear makeup
Silver flecked hair finger-waved to perfection
Plum-colored rhinestone clip-on earrings . . .
Her only fineries in fifty-two years on the farm
She's suffering no more
The smell of roses overtake wafting aromas of
Country hams   cakes   pies   platters of fried
chicken
Family and neighbors
Pray   eat   sing
Amen, sister Florence

Kenova

Nicole Yurcaba

(Third place poetry, *Skyline* contest, 2017)

You
screamed obscenities into
intimidated yet questioning
authorities whose fucking clue
emanated cluelessness.
In the emergency
room's antiseptic sterility,
you mapped anger,
the drop, the night's training mission,
dictated by elevated powers
who scheduled the exercise,
insanely, for a night
when the moon sipped
steeped cottonwood bark
and contracted into a witching hour
of authorities who rejected
that well-packed parachutes
refused opening, that epic men
separated into irreconcilable halves
when tense lines, hell-bent,
severed those who dared crossing.

Winter Dance: A Shepherd's Lament

Michael McLeod

(Third place poetry, Blue Ridge Writers Chapter contest, VWC, 2017)

The full moon shines through naked trees,
Robbed of their foliage by a bitter breeze.

The early morning sun flitters in from above,
And I cast a sad eye on this dog that I love.

Dancing shadows massage the old dog,
As she basks in the warmth of a smoldering log.

White under-carriage and four white feet,
She sleeps on her back and chases her sheep.

Light gently washes her from place-to-place
First on her tail, then on her face.

Then back it goes, in a graceful arc
A ballet of shadows, now light, now dark.

A day fast approaches when I know I must part
With this dog of my dreams, this piece of my heart.

A new dog is here, he lies at my feet,
He's doing the work, we didn't miss a beat.

But I'll miss my girl when it's her turn to go,
And put her out back, down under the snow.

Walking the Mount into Darknesses

Sigrid Mirabella

I've imagined this hike forever—
the narrow path running through
sumac, mock olive, sweet briar.

The trail inclines, quickens my breath,
heart beats rev-up, leg muscles flex,
elevation mutes hearing, twigs reach
for my body, laurel leaves lose singularity.

Dusk doesn't inhibit vision to perceive
the summit above where I live
below in that hollow place, farmed
by witless thought, plow and shovel.

Darkness swarms me into submission.
Here moon rises as a curved shard.
Pine trees confound direction, confuse
confidence, the scent making me drowsy.

So, I lie on the needles shed for salvation.
Bear have lain here, leaving a scent
like berries and sweat. Sleep creeps closer.
I hear deer whisper, stamp hooves, run off.

Overcome by darkness, I fall to sleep,
dream of Hawks screaming in a poet's voice,
moths cloaking my nose and mouth,
eyes woven shut by small round spiders.

Morning—I wake with coyote fur
caught in my nails and the smell
of pine cones like a taste on my tongue,
thick and medicinal.

Two of the Night

Sirius in April

Right behind me where I sleep
Is Sirius. I had no idea
This brightest star of all
Was outside my bedroom window
Twinkling there all night.

And I discovered Betelgeuse,
The super red giant,
Was there all along
Right out my kitchen window
Burning red in the dark.

With Bellatrix and bluish white Rigel,
And the three close in a row,
The whole Orion constellation
Has been within my view,
But I never knew.

It surprises and delights me.
(Everyone else probably knew it but me.)
Though they're millions of light years away,
I know the names of some stars
And how to spot them where they are.

Sure, they're not within my grasp,
But Alpha Centauri's triple star system
Is only 4.3 light years away.
And we've lately learned
An Earth-like planet orbits there.

I'd truly like to see it,
More directly than astronomers do,
But it's in Southern Hemisphere skies.

I can see Sirius and it will do,
It's only 8.6 light years away.

Writers in the Night

I know exactly the time
When our daystar slides away.
With Earth's 23.5 degree tilt
And the 1,000 miles-per-hour turn,
In might be slinging the Sun,
But it's only out of sight.

Then the light begins to change,
And a cooling wind blows in
A softer consciousness.
We writers meet to connect
And make a constellation.
Gravity holds us tight.

We gather close to share
A moment in nature.
Listening, we write,
Birdsong's signaling of night,
Resting photosynthesis of plants,
And the diminishing fierceness
Of our wilder friends.

April 5, 2010, on the Skyline Drive

BAMorris

Two shots ring out. Again.
She feels the searing pain.
He is coming toward her,
      his face an enraged blur.
He is reaching, grabbing,
      pushing, lifting, flinging
      her down the embankment.
To kill her, his intent.
When she climbs the incline,
      he waits on the skyline
      to once more pitch her,
      this stranger who is stronger,
      pitch her over the top
      into that long, steep drop.
She is fighting, fighting
      for her life, for living.
When she feels she can
      not defeat this madman,
      she wakes: body shaking,
      breathless with heart pounding.
The random violence,
      with its consequence,
      that night on the mountain,
      live in Christina's pain,
      and in her friend, Tim's death,
      and the spring wind's warm breath.

PROSE NONFICTION

We the People (The Fourth Branch of Government)

Jack Trammell

(A précis of the 2016 book *The Fourth Branch of Government: We the People*, coauthored with Guy Terrell)

The Fourth Branch of Government represents the genuine will and power of the people. Although some refer to the Fourth Branch as the media, the collective states, or special interest groups, the truth is that only "we the people" are the *other* branch of government that permits it to function fairly and who have ultimate say over what destiny we will pursue. The Fourth Branch, as defined in this essay, has always existed, and it is, in fact, a necessary precondition for modern, Western democracies of which we are the most important single example.

The same way students at divinity schools are taught to read sacred texts in their original language, we must reread the Constitution with the eyes of our Founders while examining our current situation. The Preamble to the Constitution, and the entire document, lays out a simple and straightforward description for the way the government of this new nation would operate. They began their Constitutional Convention in 1787 as citizens of a loose confederacy of states that banded together to win independence from England. The Founders at that time were the equivalent of what we refer to here as the Fourth Branch. Their goal, stated in the Preamble, was "in order to form a more perfect union." The nation then operated under the Articles of Confederation until the Constitution was ratified by the states in 1788 by enough states to initiate the current form of government as we know it.

We've seen the Fourth Branch active before, and we've also seen it under attack. McCarthyism was the most prominent example from the 1950s. The government actively worked to discredit and destroy dissent from decent citizens by labeling them *communists*. It was the confrontation of Joseph Welch, special counsel for the U. S. Army, during a hearing, that finally broke the power of Senator Joseph McCarthy, but others had been building the case against these hearings for some time so that Welch's confrontation had enough gravitas to put an end to McCarthyism. Here was an example of the Fourth Branch succeeding with the inclusion of people from both inside and outside the elected government. The Fourth Branch changes with the times. In the 1960s, to cite one example, the New Left was composed of a diverse collection of people pursuing social justice outside the structures of the three constitutional branches. Their activism was quite successful in bringing about important changes. On the other hand, the "establishment" was very much in fear of the Fourth Branch and used all branches of government and local means to attempt to control it or eliminate it. At some point in the late sixties, a majority of the nation turned against the nation's involvement in the Vietnam War, but it still took a presidential election and continued pressure by all groups, the Fourth Branch, to leave Vietnam in 1973.

More recently, the Fourth Branch suffered a series of body blows in 2016, as Americans were rocked by unexpected election results that severely divided the nation. There are still, as of this writing, accusations of voter fraud, election interference, voting rights violations, and collusion with a foreign power to sway our elections, all actively under investigation. Confidence in our system is probably at a historic low point right now. The evolution of the two-party system with rigid ideologies has driven out the very concept of compromise. Polls continue to show that the majority of voters support mostly moderate views. The result is that the Fourth Branch is again both active and persecuted, as it was in the 1960s and in other turbulent periods of our history. Active action is characterized, for example, by the grassroots opposition to the so-called "Alt Right"; the persecution is characterized by "fake news," "huge crowds," and slogans like "make America great again" (which is used to frighten the Fourth Branch into thinking we are *not* great right now). The events of the confrontational political demonstrations in Charlottesville in July and August 2017 might indeed suggest that we live in an awful and terrifying time. But also, the vast middle ground is silent because it has no way to express itself.

The Fourth Branch needs to be empowered through technology to have their voices heard. It would require a long national conversation and changes to the Constitution. Everyone participates in the Fourth Branch to some degree.

Nonetheless, we are great right now in the sense that we have all the potential and more that we have always had. The current crises might hold the kindling for a great fire for change. The Fourth Branch should be apolitical in the sense that it doesn't belong to any one group or branded ideology— it is always there for help when we care to use it. We each have a power channel in our democracy—a network of people, resources, and experiences—that is unique to us and that we can use to make our voice heard. People are increasingly angry, motivated, scared, and ready to get involved. The time of the Fourth Branch is here again.

Regardless of which political party or ideology you subscribe to, this time actually presents a brand-new set of unique possibilities to us. Reform of the Electoral College—an outdated, nationally gerrymandered system worthy of the Middle Ages—is as cogent as ever. An expansion of Congress to match the expansion of our citizenry is just common sense. Term limits for legislators would return us to the intended "citizen's assembly." Even the conversations about memorializing the Civil War and racism are placing us on the cusp of a significant change.

These things will not happen without the realization of the Fourth Branch, the collective will of the American people. But this will not happen if people ignore their power channels. It will not happen if we let the other three branches of government sit on their hands and talk double talk while more and more Americans fall behind. This will not happen if we let the news media be the sole watchdog.

"We the people" must finally get more involved focusing on the establishment of a workable Fourth Branch with the power to make lasting change that lifts up the majority of the nation's citizens.

A Christmas to Remember

Susan M. Lanterman

The holidays can be occasions to hand down age-old traditions—but not in my family. My grandparents emigrated from Sicily and celebrating Christmas simply involved throwing an extra chicken in the pot and a log on the fire. Being children of the Depression, my parents were "fortunate" to have second portions of soup—never mind the figgy pudding. So. my parents didn't indulge in the typical trappings of the season.

My father described one of his favorite toys as a wheel attached to a stick that he would use to run around in circles. My grandmother was the oldest of twelve children and my mother was the eldest of five. Their birth rank in the family allowed them the honor of receiving a new Christmas outfit that would be passed along to the next in a succession of siblings each year.

Unlike my parents, my sister and I had a 20-inch television screen that showed us how the rest of the world lived. Yes, Virginia, there was a Santa Claus! As children of the '50s, we would listen to our parents' tales of deprivation with a certain level of disbelief. That was, until our grandparents gave us Christmas presents like underwear with the days of the week embroidered on them and paddles with elastic strings attached to Ping-Pong–size balls. By the end of the holiday the strings had broken and we were spanked with a personal paddle throughout the coming year.

My father would procrastinate buying a Christmas tree until the only the trees left standing were holding up the "For Sale" sign. Charlie Brown, move over. After many years, my mother countered my dad's frugality by purchasing a silver tinsel tree that required placing dozens of color-coded branches into a wood "tree trunk." Her *pièce de résistance* one year was to add a multicolor disco light we stood in front of while lip-syncing Elvis Presley Christmas songs.

Every Christmas Eve, our father would oblige us by providing a white work sock to hang by our chimney—which was a stovepipe attached to our gas oven. His version of *Twas the Night Before Christmas* involved Santa squeezing down that pipe and through the oven door to deliver his presents.

I spent hours editing my letter to Santa down to a modest request for one measly gift. How could I possibly ask for a Chatty Cathy doll *and* a dollhouse? Dad would remind us each year we were the last children on Santa's ride. Our elongated stocking would be weighted down with a potato, an onion, some pocket change, and a random $2 toy.

Being the children of Depression-era parents, we were expected to always be thankful for whatever we had. So those coins in our stockings were redeemed for a fist full of penny candy and we felt somewhat luckier than the "starving children in the world," because they would have been thrilled with the prospect of one penny's worth of candy.

Early one Christmas morning, I awoke to some clamor in the kitchen. The door to our bedroom was always left open a crack to allow the heat from the stove to warm us. I slid down from my top bunk and tiptoed over in order to see Santa hard at work. Blinking back tears, I discovered my mother shoving a turkey into the oven but my limp stocking still hung nearby—empty. When I saw my father—red-handed—emptying the contents of his pockets into the stockings, the jig was up.

The following year we guilted "Santa" into putting *real* presents in our stockings, but he complied without consulting our wish list. We found a harmonica and plastic flute crammed in amongst the vegetables. We inflicted as much tonal discord as we could, hoping Santa's little helper would pay attention to our ransom notes next Christmas to ensure a little *peace on earth*.

We often participated in reenacting the Christmas story at church—bringing baby Jesus gifts of "gold, Frankenstein, and fur." There came a time when our irreverence got us demoted to nonspeaking farm animals. We were then relegated to performing this holiday ritual in the privacy of our home. My father joined in, starring as one of the wise guys—ever the jokester, he dressed as Groucho Marx or a singing drag queen.

When I had my own family, I accepted the role of Mrs. Claus with vigor. Like the Chinese New Year, I had an annual theme. One was the Year of the Fruitcake. I concocted a sleighful of inedible goodies—molding chocolates, caramelizing popcorn, baked fruitcake, and Italian cookies that would break a molar. My *pièce dé resistance* was constructing a gingerbread house that collapsed under a heavy accumulation of white frosting. In the Year of the Crossed-Stitch, every family member was outfitted with clothes created on my first Singer sewing machine: boys' coveralls that looked more like bloomers, bathrobes constructed out of towels, and monogramed underwear (helpful in case you got in an accident and needed to be identified). You can imagine the lack of support I received when in the Year of the Yarn, I created itchy wool hats that could have doubled as scarves due to my enthusiastic knitting. But all were made with love.

Last year my parents moved out of their home of fifty years, and, like a Charles Dickens character, I hoped to discover some of my childhood memories from Christmases past in their dusty attic. Maybe I'd come across a box containing the stripped silver branches or our first "real" toy— a pinball game (still missing a leg), or the wreath decorated in petrified lollipops. But there, tucked in a box, was a string of holiday bells I had cut out of construction paper for my parents long ago in Kindergarten with my name written mostly in backward letters. Realizing my parents had saved my childhood artwork for so many years put my memories into perspective. It reminded me of the old Shaker hymn, "Tis a gift to be simple."

And it doesn't take a village of elves to provide a gift from the heart.

Vendimia in the Ribeira Sacra in Galicia

Stephen Bush

(This essay first appeared in the 2016 Cyberworld Publishing anthology *The Good Life in Galicia.*)

From January to October life in the Ribeira Sacra region of Galicia, Spain, revolves around its vineyards and the grapes they are to produce. And Vendimia, the grape harvest, is the frenzy of picking and crushing, followed by the eating and drinking and fiestas (parties) in the afternoons, which end each year's season of the grapes. Vendimia starts when the grapes are ready to be picked, and the starting date can vary by over a month from year to year. In the last ten years it has started as early as late August and as late as the second of October.

Many hundreds of villages and a dozen small towns lie within the river valleys of the Sil and Miño rivers that compose what is known as the Ribeira Sacra, and their vineyards are of great importance to every community. Most grapes are still grown on small plots of land. A family may have one vineyard plot or many vineyards scattered around a village or town. The distribution of land belonging to a family is the result of inheritances and marriages over the centuries, and the modern result is a region filled with a picturesque patchwork of vineyards and vegetable gardens (huertas), as well as many untended plots of land that are returning to the forest, which link the small villages and towns, each with its own collection of ancient stone houses.

In recent years there has been some amalgamation of the small vinyas into large vineyards and major winemakers have emerged, but they still account for only a small part of the grapes harvested and wine made.

Vines in the Ribeira Sacra are mostly of the red Mencia variety, with the white Godello being the most common white wine grape grown. Other varieties are far less important. All vines receive a lot of personal care throughout the period from January to October, with pruning, clearing, spraying, and more clearing and spraying occurring as the season progresses, right up to two or three weeks before the grapes are harvested. All this work is done by hand, and for many vineyard owners it is important that the pruning and care of the vines is done in tune with the cycles of the moon. The narrow roads that wind into the river valleys become extra busy on what are believed to be the auspicious days. The vineyard workers, usually the owners or a relative, park where they can on the narrow and often steep roads. Once they have found a parking place, they often have some distance still to go and climb the rocky paths, which usually are only wide enough for one person to walk them at a time, to their vineyards.

Most Ribeira Sacra vines are grown on rock-walled terraces hand built over the centuries. These terraces climb the steep sides of the canyons of the Sil, in places up to a 600 meters deep, and the Miño, nearly 400 meters deep. Many small plots are only reachable on foot and there are a few vineyards in the canyon of the river Sil that can only be reached by boat.

The rivers Sil and Miño were dammed in the 1960s to provide hydroelectric power. Before that the canyons fell to an even greater depth. Many villages and vineyards were lost when the valleys were flooded. The depth and shape of the winding river canyons create numerous micro climates that are warmer and wetter than the surrounding, higher, land, and this is one of the secrets of the Riberia Sacra as a wine-growing region. Another secret is that, though the region is full of rock, the soil on the river banks is rich—thick, damp, alluvial soil full of organic matter and nutrients that, over the millenniums, has washed down from the surrounding hills, hills that are nearly all still covered in natural pine forest and patches of Spanish Oak, not depleted farmland, so the soils of the valley vineyards are replenished constantly.

Looking at the valley walls, the pattern of still-cultivated vineyards, seems haphazard till you learn that those that face north get less sun and colder winds and produce fewer grapes and those that face south get more sun and the warm winds and produce more. Many productive vineyards have fallen out of cultivation as the growers have concentrated on the best-yielding plots.

On the terraces the season's work normally begins in January with pruning. It is midwinter and the mornings in the valleys are misty and cold. There may even be frosts and occasional snowfalls on the hills. Few vineyards are accessible by machinery that is not carried on the back of a man, and pruning a vineyard may take a man a few hours if it is small or several men a few days if it is large. Experience will tell the pruner how each branch on each vine must be cut to ensure the most grapes and the best harvest for the coming season.

The Ribeira Sacra is one of several recognized Denominations of Origin in Galicia. It became an official Denomintión de Origen in 1997, but the area has been home to vineyards since it was under Roman rule. These Denominations are similar to the Appelations of France, and in accredited vineyards the care of the vines is closely monitored not only by the vineyard owner but also by the Denomination body. Not all vineyards in the region are accredited. It is a choice. And most are not. And many of those that are not accredited produce wonderful wines.

Grape growing and wine production were introduced to the area by the ancient Romans and it is said that the legendary spiced Vinos de Amandi were made here and shipped to Rome, along with the lampreys fished out of the river Miño, to be served at the table of the emperor. The Amandi area in the Sil valley today produces some of the region's best wines.

Also with January's pruning comes the work of clearing the weeds and vine shoots that have grown up between the vines in the last few months. The clearing used to be done by digging by hand between the vines, but now it's done with machines; small tillers, and brush cutters or, unfortunately, increasingly with herbicide. Today many of the owners of small vineyards, particularly the younger owners, live in larger nearby towns, and for them spraying herbicide is a way to do in an hour or two a job that might otherwise take a day or two. And in larger vineyards it saves many hours of labor that must be paid for. But many local winegrowers disapprove of it.

Once the initial clearing and pruning are done, there is a pause in activity until the vines flower. The flowering occurs in late April or early May. Grapevines have little need for bees or insects, as their flowers are usually hermaphroditic, what are called perfect flowers, which can self-pollinate. The flowers are tiny and green and barely noticeable. The cycle of the grape's life from the flowering of the vine to the ripening of the fruit will vary in length with the weather, and the activity of caring for the vines will also vary. Dry weather or heavy rains will affect not only the growth of the grapes but also the times and frequency for clearing between the vines and later for spraying with fungicide.

The Ribeira Sacra is said to take its name from the eighteen monasteries and hermitages that were founded along the then often-inaccessible river valleys in the early Middle Ages—between the eighth and twelfth centuries. It is also said to have been the monks in those monasteries who replanted the vineyards for their own consumption and maintained the grape-growing and wine-producing tradition up to modern times. One of the best surviving examples of these monasteries is San Estevo de Ribas de Miño, which sits high above the river Miño on the road to Lalin (http://www.turismo.gal/ficha-recurso?cod_rec=15683).

This is a romantic story, but the area has been occupied continuously from Neolithic times and is home to the remains of pre-Roman Celtic villages. And it would be strange if the Romans did not leave some knowledge of grape growing and winemaking behind with the local communities.

Nestling in sheltered valleys, rooted in the rich soils and fueled by the heat of summer, the grapes grow rapidly. Regular spraying with fungicide, often still the natural copper sulphate, is necessary to ensure the grapes flourish. In some years the wild vines will grow bunches of tiny grapes in abundance but in other years the wild unsprayed vines will produce nothing. Fungus is a serious problem in the region. Some vineyards spray by the cycles of the moon and others do not, and sometimes spraying more often will not achieve as much as a neighbor's less-frequent spraying. In the steep twisting valleys growing conditions can vary in short distances, and in hard years production can also vary considerably.

Localized intense hailstorms and unexpected frosts can also occur to ravage crops in an area.

But in most years the Ribeira Sacra is generous to its wine growers, and by August the vines will be laden with large, firm bunches of fruit. A final cutting back of the excess foliage by some growers will add a bit more to the size and flavor of the grapes and make the picking easier, but not many do it.

All the grapes in the Ribeira Sacra are harvested by hand, each cluster cut carefully from the vine and placed in a plastic crate or bucket. Not so many years ago these were still special baskets made of woven strips of wood and shaped to fit snugly on the shoulders, but with the rim projecting over a man's head, making it easy to grasp. When the crates are full, which will be over twenty kilos of grapes, they will be carried on a man's shoulders, sometimes directly to the crusher, but usually carried to the place where they are to be collected and loaded onto a boat or a trailer or tractor for transport to the bodega or winery. In larger vineyards on the steep slopes the baskets are carried to the rails, which take the full crates down the slope.

In vineyards that are certified for Denominatión production, the time to begin the harvest is decided by the controlling body based on testing of the grapes, and the day decided on will be a guide for the start of the harvest for everyone, accredited or not, who is harvesting in the area.

Finally, somewhere between late August and early October, the vineyards come alive for the harvest. In the days before crates and buckets for the grapes are set ready in large vineyards, pallets and empty trailers are parked on whatever available parking area is nearby, and family and friends prepare themselves. Early in the morning on weekends normally empty roads are now full of cars driving out of the nearby towns and cities. Most are full of people, some pull covered trailers. Vendimia has begun.

The harvest is known as Vendimia. It is not just about picking grapes, though that is why it exists, it is about families and friends coming together to work from early morning until midafternoon and then, tired from a day bent over in the heat and carrying the full, heavy baskets of grapes up and down steep paths, gathering together in the small bodegas in the vineyards or nearby in someone's home for a meal. Grandmothers and mothers and children who are too old or too young to help in the harvest will have cooked for much of the morning, ready for the hungry grape pickers to come in and eat. In a small vineyard the picking may only be for a day and will end with the meal. It will be a large meal, with several courses of traditional Galician food, and their own wine and homemade brandies, a meal that is a celebration that goes into the late afternoon. After the meal there may be some work done, but it is not necessary.

In a large vineyard the workers and their families will be invited to a fiesta after the harvest is finished, a fiesta that will begin with a large lunch and go into the night, possibly moving to a local café before the last worker finally surrenders to the need to sleep.

But wait, Vendimia may be the end of the grape growing season, but in the days and weeks that follow, it will be the winemakers' time to make the wine, and the winemaking season will have begun in the bodegas and wineries, large and small.

Midnight Mountain Birth

Elizabeth Doyle Solomon

(First place nonfiction, *Skyline* contest, 2017)

Shannon, with the one curly horn, was the most gentle of my dairy goat herd. Among the seven milkers, her Alpine heritage gave us two gallons a day. She was heavy with spring kids, her white sides bulging.

It was early March in the mountains of our seventeen-acre farm, Shamrock Ridge. Wildflowers popped up beneath the snow, especially the early twin-leaf, with its single white bloom, and the lavender hepaticas, with their rosettes of purple leaves.

I had been down the mountain every day, checking on Shannon's progress. Today, four-year old daughter Molly came with me. "How many babies will she have, Mom?" she asked. Children grow up quickly on a farm, see life and death as natural. Molly was always asking questions, and I did my best to answer truthfully.

I put her little hands on Shannon's white-furred side. "Now just push gently, Molly, right here, and you'll feel one kid's head."

"Oooh," Molly crooned. "I feel a baby!" She then went to Shannon's other side, and did the same thing. "Mom! I think she's gonna have two!"

Mariah, my Nubian doe, had already kidded in late February—triplet does, all girls—the best a dairy goat breeder could ask for. Two days later, Moira, my other Alpine doe, dropped twins, a doe and a buck. I was there in the kidding barn for both births, ready with iodine, scissors, and warm blankets for the babies. Up the steep hill I climbed each time (always after midnight), cradling the newborns. I had a large appliance box filled with oat straw beneath the kitchen table.

It's important to milk the mothers immediately after birthing, when their udders fill for that first nutritious colostrum, which ensures newborn kids a healthy start. I had soda bottles ready with black nipples that fit over the tops. Each time, with both Mariah's and Moira's kiddings, Molly had been asleep. In the mornings, she always asked, "Mom, why didn't you wake me?"

Both my daughters, aged four and nine, enjoyed bottle-feeding the babies. They watched from the fence as the sure-footed little kids leapt and pranced in the pasture, sometimes dancing sideways. Newborn goat kids are hilarious, but they are also sweet and docile, can be trained like a cat to an indoor litter box, and like a dog to a leash!

It was now, by this time, March tenth. I was milking Moira and Mariah twice a day, and feeding bottles to five kids, five times a day. The steady supply of goats' milk assured my family of daily glasses. I was baking six loaves of bread a week, using buttermilk left by churning cream to butter. There was so much milk—four gallons a day!—that I also had enough to make yogurt and soft goats' cheese.

After morning milking on March eleventh, I went into the upper pasture to the hen house to collect eggs and feed my flock of Rhode Island red hens and one bully rooster, whom the girls had named Bossy. The sky was a heavy metal-gray, and the air felt like snow. I looked for Shannon on the mixed snow and grass slopes, but could not spot her.

After carrying my basket of ten fat, brown eggs inside, I decided now was the time to check on Shannon. Molly was playing with her favorite dolls, feeding them a pretend breakfast.

"Do you want to come with me to check on Shannon?" Wow, did she ever! She slipped on her winter jacket with its fur-trimmed hood, put on mittens and snowboots. By the time we walked downhill to the kidding barn, it was snowing—small flakes and falling fast—which meant it was going to snow a lot and last a long time.

Shannon was standing at the keyhole feeder, munching on sweet, dry alfalfa hay. Goats will not eat hay from the ground as cows do. They are finicky eaters, and like their meals dry and safely off the barn floor. The first thing I saw about Shannon was that she had "dropped," just as a woman does in the days before giving birth. There was also the tell-tale mucous plug, hanging from her back end.

"Mom, look! I think she's getting ready!" Molly's sharp little blue eyes saw everything I saw. She moved slowly and cautiously, closer to our expectant mother, and put her two short arms as far as they would reach around Shannon's bulging sides.

"It's OK, Shannon," Molly crooned to the waiting mother. "Your babies will soon be here!" Shannon bleated softly, raised her head from the feeder, and softly nuzzled Molly's cheek. "She kissed me, Mom! She knows I love her!" Molly and I sat on a tied-up bale of alfalfa hay. "Well, Molly Doodle," I said, using her pet name, "what do you think should be our next step?" She had been through this process before. "We need to make her bed softer, Mom." I looked at the kidding stall with its oat straw, somewhat flattened now by Shannon's heavy body.

"Yes, indeed, that's my farm girl," I replied to Molly. I climbed the loft ladder and called out, "Step inside the stall, honey. You'll be safer there when I throw this bale down."

With Molly in a safe place, I threw the bale of oat straw down. I cut the baling twine, and Molly wound it around her arm as she had seen me do a dozen times. She handed me the small ring of twine, and I hung it from a nail where other twine had collected. "Waste not, want not," I echoed the creed my own father had so often quoted to me growing up. Molly and I spread half of the sweet-smelling oat straw in the stall. As we finished, Shannon sniffed it and laid herself down.

"I think these babies will come tonight, Molly. What do you think?"

Excitement was in her eyes and voice as she clapped her hands. "Oh Mom, yes! And we'll be right here to see her babies born, won't we?" Molly hugged me and then went over to Shannon and hugged her. Shannon licked Molly's cheek as if to say, "Thank you for taking such good care of me."

We trudged back up the steep hill to the farmhouse. There were already three inches, snow on snow. As the old-time farmers told me, "when there's snow on the ground, there will be more snow." By suppertime, there were six inches! Spring in these mountains near the West Virginia border was always late in coming. We were often still using blankets on our beds after May the first.

After a supper of homemade soup and my fresh-baked bread, my two girls fed the ever-hungry goat babies their last bottle of the day. These soda bottles had to be heated slowly, half-submerged in a pot of water on the gas stove.

I read another chapter of the famous classic, *Heidi*, (the goat girl) to my daughters before they went to sleep in their bunk beds. Molly slept in her clothes, so to be ready the minute I called her. Shawn was not as enthusiastic about seeing the actual births. She was content to see the goat kids *after* all the mess was over!

Girls asleep, I worked on my ever-arriving poems in the night's quiet, soft shushing of snow coating our farmhouse's seamed-tin roof. There was so much to tell since I wrote my first poem at age eleven. Who could have told, New Orleans city girl that I was, I'd be a dairy goat farmer at age thirty-two? I thought of my Oklahoma-prairie Grandma, birthing and raising eleven children beginning in 1900 with a woodstove to be filled in winter, a hand-cranked bucket at the well, and two cows to be milked in the barn. Sometimes we skip a generation, I thought, in taking after our ancestors. Not one of Grandma's children had chosen to live on a farm. It was only I, one of thirty-odd grandchildren, who had this fascination for the earth and farm animals.

At eleven-thirty, I pulled on a hooded parka, slipped into the knee-high boots, lit the wick on an oil lantern, and made the trek through deep snow to the kidding barn. The rest of my herd, including 200 pound buck Mister Bill, were all safely chomping away on their cuds in the upper barn with its row of keyhole feeders. The loft was packed with bales of alfalfa hay. It was a good feeling to know that my husband and I had built sturdy barns and secured the winter's food supply for our goat family before the snow began to fall.

I opened the kidding barn door and closed it behind me, setting my lantern on the post hook above Shannon's stall. She bleated softly to greet me as I observed her situation. She was standing, in the position does prefer at onset of labor! Shannon was pushing, and breathing heavily. Great puffs of moisture-laden air came from her mouth as she gave these powerful pushes. I had to wake up Molly!

Grabbing the oil lantern, I quickly closed the barn door and worked my way back up the steep hill, soft snow squeaking and scrunching beneath my boots. In the kitchen I had bottles and nipples ready. Five goat kids lay tangled in the oat-straw box beneath the table, blissfully asleep. I tip-toed into the girls' bedroom and woke Molly. Then going to our room, I touched my husband's shoulder, which woke him like a fire bell! He dressed in a flash, but it wasn't fast enough for Molly. "Come *on*, Daddy—hurry!"

In the kitchen I grabbed my birthing kit, which contained iodine, sterilized scissors, clean rags, and latex gloves, just in case I had to apply my midwife skills. Molly carried the milk pail, and my husband had blankets and the lantern. I needed all the help I could get with the birth, cleaning Shannon and the kids, then transporting everything back up the hill.

As we opened the kidding barn door, Shannon moaned softly as if to say, "I'm glad you're here." By the lantern's light, we saw the battery-operated clock on the barn wall with its hands at midnight. Shannon's first kid, white as snow, dropped softly into the oat straw. It was a buck. While Shannon licked her newborn, I applied iodine and cut his cord. Molly sat in the stall and cradled the baby in her lap. I will never forget that scene: my little Molly in her red, fur-trimmed jacket and hood, looking adoringly at Shannon's midnight kid!

About twenty minutes later, Shannon gave one last enormous push and the second kid dropped, also a buck. He was much smaller than his twin brother, but both of them seemed to be strong and healthy. I applied iodine and cut his cord too while Shannon licked him clean, his white fur glistening. Molly now had the two newborns in her lap, while I used the fresh rags in my birthing kit to make the mother presentable.

"Mom, they're so soft!" Molly murmured as the kids curious lips tickled her cheeks and hands. We three sat in the oat straw inside a circle of lantern light and marveled in silence and awe at this miracle of nature.

197

Shannon's udder was swollen full, and I knew this was the next most important step: to milk her colostrum. We led her to the milking stand, filled the feed bucket with a mixture of oats and molasses, and congratulated this hard-working mother. Shannon's twin streams pinged into the pail, a sound old as Time itself. We put fresh alfalfa in the keyhole feeder, and left the curly-horned doe to her well-deserved rest.

Falling snow sparkled in the lantern's light as we climbed the steep hill to Shamrock Ridge farmhouse. I held one kid, Molly held the second smaller one, and Wynn carried the milk pail, lantern, and my birthing kit. Molly ran into the house to her bedroom, squealing to the sleeping mound beneath blankets, "Shawn, Shawn—wake up! We've got two more baby goats in the kitchen!"

What pandemonium enfolded us all! Older babies woke to greet the newborns with much bleating and wagging of short little tails. I used a funnel to pour colostrum into two soda bottles, then heated them to mother's temperature on the stove. Shawn fed one baby, and Molly, the other. I had enough of this "mother's first milk" to freeze some, in case another doe birthed without an ample supply.

In the birthing journal for that spring, I added Shannon's name, date, and the time. The girls named the twin bucks that night: Buckwheat for the larger twin, and Little Kernel for his smaller brother. We now had seven babies in the large straw-filled box beneath the kitchen table!

That wondrous, snowy-midnight birth, when Shannon of the one curly horn dropped two buck kids into oat straw of our kidding stall, happened over forty-one years ago. The little girls have grown into women, and those buck kids all went to loving homes when they were weaned. My dairy-farm days are long behind me, but the memories of Shamrock Ridge Farm are tattooed into my brain, words continuing to ink the pages of today's stories and poems.

First Dance

Roger Tolle

(First place nonfiction, Blue Ridge Writers Chapter contest, VWC, 2017)

On a hot Friday night in the summer of 1975, four of us from Concert Dance Company—Robb, Kitty, Deb, and I—strolled into 1270, one of only two gay dance bars in Boston. We arrived to take over the floor, as we often did, just as the music began around 9:00 p.m. We wasted no time filling the dark, empty expanse with our oversized strutting, twirling, swinging, bopping, and leaping. The smooth wood floor provided a springboard to toss ourselves into each other's arms, roll over each other's backs, groove into and out of synchronized steps, and slide on our knees in an extravagant demonstration of bravado, two years ahead of John Travolta in *Saturday Night Fever*. We laughed, and grunted, and whistled at each other's antics and sang along with tunes we recognized.

After an hour of our weekend unwinding, we all kissed each other goodnight, and Kitty and Deb scurried off to their apartments for a good night's sleep. They had no interest in the next stage of the weekend's rituals that drew Robb and me in like a pair of moths. They didn't want to hang around to be crowded out by the disapproving stares of the young men who claimed this sanctuary as gay-male-only from 10:00 p.m. on.

Robb and I had an unspoken agreement to give each other space once "the boys" arrived in sufficient numbers, so we could shift from our free-form dancing into the more strictly defined movements of the disco style, a movement language that we each adapted for maximum seduction value.

On my own, I reined in my dancing only a little, even with the available space dwindling rapidly. I believed that being upfront with my movement skill and my deft handling of rhythms gave me a better chance of attracting the attention of a man I would be interested in—a man who pulsed with the same aliveness and sensual joy that I did.

As the hour got later and the music got louder, I repositioned my dancing near the entrance of the club. I wasn't quite ready to give up, but I told myself I was on my way out. Here at the bottleneck of men oozing in and out of the club, my bobbing body added one more impediment to the flow. Here it was that a lovely boy collided with me as he tripped into the club with his friends.

We both flailed in surprise but found our footing again quickly, as our startled hands latched onto each other for support. And then our eyes met. And something happened for which I was unprepared. I hadn't intended to lose my edge, nor my constructed image. But in that moment, I connected to him from a part of me that had no outer form.

That moment was interrupted when he grabbed my hand and pulled me toward the center of the densely packed dance floor, abandoning his friends without a backward glance. My rising spirits pulsed new energy into my dancing, and I matched his rhythm and style.

As the first song ended, I yelled, "What's your name?"

"What?" he yelled back.

I cupped my hands around my mouth and yelled louder, into his ear. "Name."

"Oh." He leaned in enough for me to smell the freshness in his hair and cupped his hands around my ear. "Tom. What's yours?"

"Roger," I yelled back and smiled.

A few minutes later, I again cupped my hands around his ear and added, "I really like dancing with you."

Coordinating his movements with the beat of the music, his mouth moved and his hands waved back and forth between us in the well-understood gesture of, "Me, too."

Without any further conversation, we spent the next hour moving in harmony. My body seemed to know exactly where his weight would land on each beat. My fingers sought and intertwined with his. I tuned in constantly to whether he was leading me or following me, and how quickly and how often that changed.

Tom matched my dancing with equal attention and met my eyes with a mischievous grin. In this crowded and noisy environment, it was not easy to get enough distance to see his whole body, but I could see he was my size. We matched each other perfectly—the same wavy dark brown hair and flushed pale skin, deep-set hazel eyes with long black lashes, intensely focused gaze, untempered exclamations of delight in each new disco hit the DJ played.

Later, both of us sweating and breathing hard, we bubbled out of the bar and rushed for my old, clunky, black Volvo. As soon as we fell into the wide front seat, we kissed and grabbed at each other. That dilapidated hulk of a car that usually offended my sense of style now seemed the perfect backdrop for our lusty groping.

I had to push Tom's hands away repeatedly to drive, although I really didn't want to. I was thrilled that he pulled himself up close to me for the entire time it took to cross the Charles River. At the Cambridge apartment where I was housesitting that month, we tumbled out of the car and raced for the door, laughing and bouncing off each other, unaware there might be neighbors sleeping. As soon as we fell through the doorway, we dove onto the high four-poster bed that dominated the tiny studio, pulling at each other's sticky clothes. With our pants still hobbling our ankles, our freshly exposed bellies finally made sliding contact, and sent both of us over the edge.

Saturday morning, I woke up with Tom's nose touching mine, and just a hint of his sweet breath in my nostrils. I leaned in and kissed the tops of his eyelids, then laid back on the pillow to watch his long lashes flutter open and a big grin grow to fill his face.

Then I kissed him on the lips, full and long, savoring the rich emotional sweetness that was contained in the soft flesh. Our early morning cuddling awakened a fierce and mutual arousal. It was simple, adolescent, filled with youthful urgency.

The second time we woke up, faces only inches from each other again, we finally began to talk.

"Good morning, beautiful," I said to his slightly spacey smile.

Out of his fog of afterglow, and with half-awake lips, he somehow managed to find a lilt in his voice. "Good morning, gorgeous."

"What's on your agenda for the day?" I asked, hopefully.

"You," is all he answered.

I melted inside, and, for a long moment, lost myself in his eyes.

"Shower?" He asked.

"Good idea."

In the luxurious, walk-in alcove, the fancy sea sponge and bar of lilac-scented soap grabbed our attention. They quickly proved their potential for boy-body worship. If tile is uncomfortable for long periods of kneeling, we didn't notice.

Once we had dried each other off, we picked out fresh shorts and T-shirts from my stack on the dresser, leaving our Friday night clothes, still damp with sweat, crumpled in a pile on the floor. He looked really sexy in my clothes, as we strolled down to Harvard Square for a late breakfast.

Between bites of pancakes, we filled each other in on what our lives were like, how much we loved our respective artistic disciplines, how it felt to be an artist and learning to live as one. My rehearsal schedule with Concert Dance Company had just slipped into a late-summer pause. I was still planning on going to the company's studio to take company class starting Monday, but I made it perfectly clear he was welcome to spend as much of the weekend with me as he wanted.

He was on summer break from classes at the Massachusetts College of Art and felt compelled to go into one of their studios to work on a project that he hoped to complete before school resumed in the fall. He gushed to me about a wall-sized collage piece, and how important finishing it this month was to him.

"I just have to get the colors right, first. It's still not right even with all the stuff I put on it this week. I really need to get back into the studio soon." But then a tantalizing twist of his lips betrayed his stated intentions, and he added, "But maybe it can wait till Monday."

I grinned back, broadly. "Then maybe we can head back to the apartment?"

All through that weekend, we interrupted our bed time only to shower or go get food. When we had sex, I merged inside him, feeling what he was feeling, physically, emotionally and energetically. When he giggled, or twisted away, I pulled him closer. When I tickled him, he just laughed. We gave ourselves over to each exquisite connection.

From that first weekend, our life together left as little separate time as possible. If we hadn't had somewhere else we needed to go each day, we would have stayed glued together in bed. But our individual needs to reconnect with our artistic endeavors outweighed even this enthralling new love.

As another week came and went, we began to make meals and do laundry together, we went shopping in the farmers' market, took walks around Harvard Square. I shared my new boyfriend joy with the other dancers in the company, and he talked about me with his college friends.

My dancing began to reflect this euphoric mood. Without a calm center, balancing got harder, but I cared less about it, too. I flitted around the studio, barely touching the ground. Never having felt myself a particularly athletic dancer, my excited body now found pleasure in the most athletic movement phrases.

Back at the apartment, Tom and I cuddled with each other as we talked at length about art. We read to each other—one day poetry, another day essays on being an artist—sharing big dreams and untested confidence. We even read the news aloud, our cocoon of caresses insulating us from really registering the world's horrors.

We fell asleep and woke again in each other's arms. We scrunched our noses at the musty residue of our sex. We formulated at great length, and with much debate, our own theory about the art and science of snuggling. And, eventually, we shared with each other the realization that we'd found in each other a soul mate—the identical twin from whom we had been separated at birth. When we looked in the mirror together, as we sometimes did just to confirm what we felt, we saw ourselves in each other. When we strolled through the streets of Cambridge or Boston, laughing and hanging all over each other, we pretended we were twin brothers. In those days before gay liberation really took hold, our look-alike presentation was a good cover, we thought, for the irrepressible glow of our infatuation.

I merged so deeply with him, it was magical. So intense. So right. I could not imagine not being with him and loving him for the rest of my life. I assumed he felt the same for me.

One afternoon at the beginning of September, physically drained after rehearsal, but emotionally excited and ready for another evening of surrender to the sensual pleasure of being with him, I drove over to pick him up at his apartment. We never spent time at his place. With his roommate there, it lacked the privacy we wanted. We were just intending to have a last night at the spacious Cambridge apartment we had been enjoying that August—a final night of being alone together—before I had to move back into my tiny room in the huge, ramshackle house in Brookline I would be sharing the rest of the year with a whole community of struggling artists and destitute students.

When I got to his apartment, though, his roommate came to the door to answer the bell.

"Tom isn't coming," she told me.

"What?" I didn't understand.

"He couldn't come down to tell you himself, because the whole thing has become too intense. He couldn't handle it. He can't come with you tonight."

"What do you mean, too intense?" My efforts to keep my voice from climbing up out of my throat weren't working. "Is he under too much pressure from school or something?"

She hesitated. Her narrow eyes pinched tighter and she bit her lower lip. She was not comfortable delivering the unexpected and disappointing message.

"The only information he gave me was that he just had to call the whole thing off. It was getting too intense."

When she closed the door quickly without another word, I stood there for a long moment, stunned. Then I staggered back to my old, boxy, black Volvo sedan, slid into the driver's seat, and pulled the door firmly closed beside me. I gulped in one big breath. I paused, eyes wide. Then I watched as my mind separated from my body, observing what happened next from some inner distance. I filled the inside of that car with sounds I didn't know I knew how to make. I wailed so hard, my stomach cramped. I couldn't focus my eyes. The wailing eventually slowed down, but then I sobbed again so hard it hurt my throat. I coughed in fits of hacking, and gasped for air. Inside that safe and soundproof coffin, I watched as a younger part of me suffocated and died.

My mind grabbed for explanations. What did that mean, "too intense"? Wasn't that the point of a passion such as ours? Wasn't intensity what drove us to seek connection with each other through the vulnerable sharing of sex? Hadn't we both said this relationship was the most beautiful and satisfying experience we'd ever had? Wasn't intensity what everyone longed for?

As that day gave way to the next, and the weeks disappeared in blurry succession, I ran these questions over and over in my mind. I drained my fellow dancers with my obsessive rehashing. I burst into tears at the most inappropriate moments in rehearsal and had to run outside to catch my breath before I could go on. With no previous experience to prepare me for this level of emotional pain, I just wallowed in it.

I didn't hear from Tom again. He wouldn't answer my calls. The sudden loss of the relationship became a dark and heavy presence I could push aside only partially. It would revisit me whenever I had time to rest—while watching the other dancers work on sections of the choreography, or even more intensely once I was alone in the car on the way home from rehearsal. It was a struggle to get back to the studio each day.

One bitter Tuesday morning in November, I trudged into the big drafty studio, bundled up in layers of tights, sweats, socks, leg warmers, sweaters, and even a scarf around my neck. I began rolling on the floor, groaning and stretching, until everyone was ready to begin our daily class. On some mornings, Deb would lead us through a free-flowing modern dance warm-up. But on this morning, Kitty led us through a well-constructed ballet barre, with frequent changes in tempo that helped us get warm quickly and deep down to the core. She wanted us to work not only the big outer muscles, but also to stretch out the intrinsic muscles around the spine. Although I had already been working these past two years on lengthening and realigning my central axis, this morning's efforts demanded even more core lengthening. The work was hard, but it felt real and important, and, I sensed, also touched into the tension that was holding my grief.

At the end of the hour-and-a-half class, with our muscles warm and minds now awake, Barbara, our artistic director, asked us to run through "Cartouche," a dance we had recently learned from New York choreographer Phoebe Neville. This dark and slow-moving piece was set to some particularly ponderous music of Henry Purcell, tympani and trumpets at a funereal pace that only underscored my mood.

The piece is for two dancers. Since the roles are not gender specific, all of us were learning both parts. Rehearsals involved the whole company, and each time we ran it, we would be paired up in different combinations.

This morning I took the role we affectionately called the "bottom." That meant I started the dance lying face down on the floor. Robb, as my "top," stood on my back, one foot on my sacrum and one in my mid back. With his solid 160 pounds of muscle weight, it was a lot for my body to handle. Robb's wide feet distributed his weight well, and for the first six minutes of the dance, my attention focused on nothing but breathing and letting my body be flattened on the floor. I forgot my emotional pain.

Halfway through the dance, Robb executed his slow-motion dismount and spread out on his belly. Then I climbed up awkwardly onto his back, worked my way through some proud and architectural gestures, eventually tightening into a crouch, where, without any conscious intention, my body began filling each posture with the passion of unresolved feelings. In the final triumphant and gruesome gesture, hovering over Robb like a vulture, my grief found its form. My gut squeezed up through my heart, my jaw clenched, and a tear fell on the back of Robb's head.

As the music ended and we all broke the tension at the end of the dance, I stepped carefully off Robb's back. Deb glanced over at me as she got off her perch on Kitty's back. "Roger, are you okay?"

I stood there, my body beginning to shake violently. I couldn't speak, still full as I was with the dawning awareness of what my body had just done.

There was silence in the studio for several long moments. Then, in a gesture of fatherly tenderness he would never show me again, Robb pulled me back onto the floor and held me in a tight, full-body curl. Barbara simply said, "Let's take a break, everyone."

As the other dancers ambled over to retrieve warmer clothes and cups of coffee, she came up to Robb and me on the floor, took my face in her small, bony hands, and looked me straight in the eyes to be sure she had my full attention. "That's how I want you to dance that piece every time. Nothing less."

I nodded, wiped my nose, and gave Robb a quick thank-you hug, then got up and, still shaking, began wrapping myself in layers of warm clothes. The emotional roller coaster I'd been riding had finally found its way back to earth. I'd discovered how to convert emotional intensity into a way of dancing that projected both depth and power.

From then on I "owned" that dance. Whenever the company performed it, I was cast—in the role of the bottom who ends up triumphantly on top.

Over the Snowy Blue Ridge on a Moped at Night

Leonard Tuchyner

(Second place nonfiction, *Skyline* contest, 2017)

I left Harrisonburg well after I knew the home-bound traffic would be slight. Old Sol had already set, but the Western skies glowed a dusky silvery light. It was cold and cloudy. Snow was predicted. Low overcast skies reflected ambient illumination radiating out of the city's outskirts.

"How bad can the weather get?" I asked myself. This was not really a question. I was convincing myself that I could handle whatever the weatherman could throw at me.

My home was on the eastern side of Skyline Drive, and I had important people to meet the next morning. I made the forty-five-mile trek at least once a week. However, I'd never driven a moped over the mountain in a snowstorm.

As I stepped out onto the office parking lot, I considered my options. I wasn't sure the risks should be taken, but my legs seemed to have a mind of their own, and they walked to where my moped was chained to a tree. A few small flakes were already beginning to flutter their way down. I could turn around and camp out in my sub-office and leave before dawn the next morning. I had done so before, but what would the roads be like in the morning if we had a substantial accumulation of slippery snow? No! It would be better to get over the Blue Ridge before that had a chance to happen. Otherwise, there was no telling when I would be able to make it home. Changing my scheduled appointments would also cause a lot of problems. In addition, April, my dog, would go hungry. I didn't worry about her freezing, because she had a thick winter coat and knew how to find shelter, though she'd be sad and nervous.

Being legally blind made riding the two-wheeled vehicle particularly treacherous at night, when my remaining vision was minimal, but I had done that often. Even though mopeds do not require a driver's license, I often wondered what the cops would do if they realized a visually impaired person was periodically driving one over the mountain. Ordinarily, the trip took me from two to two-and-a-half hours. Just a little bit of snow or ice on the streets would make that a more difficult and time-consuming trip—all the more reason to get on my way, I reasoned.

Boy, was it cold, though there wasn't much wind. A few more isolated snowflakes were fluttering down gently through a quiet sky.

After unlocking the moped, I put the lock and chain in the panniers and ascertained that there was an extra sparkplug. Then I donned my mittens and roll-started the little one-cylinder engine.

I was out on Route 33 within five minutes. That was the highway that would take me over the Blue Ridge Mountains and on to my home in Ruckersville. The route was a straight shot, requiring only one turn, which would occur when I reached Route 29, forty-five miles away. The ground would be relatively flat until I reached the mountain, so I did not anticipate any difficulties getting to the base of the ascent. The real challenge would be getting up to the summit and then back down on the eastern side.

The problem was that those few isolated flakes of snow turned out to be a vanguard for a major winter assault. Within a few miles, I could hardly keep my eyes open through the battering that the precipitation was giving my eyeballs. Icicles were already beginning to form under my nose and onto my face mask, as vapor from my breath froze. More than once, I considered turning back, but I was young, strong, and bullheaded. I'd ridden through snow before, and I could do it again. Admittedly, I'd never done it going over a mountain.

By the time I reached the last traffic light going east out of Harrisonburg, the snow was already two inches deep. It was a fine-grained, dry ski-slope type snow. That was not a good thing for two-wheeled vehicles. I was astonished at how fast it had accumulated. There wasn't much traffic, but that which was there had packed the lanes with two sets of compressed-snow tracks that completely hid the pavement. I could feel my back wheels tending to slide to the left, so I took my feet off the pedals, stuck them out on both sides to act like ski runners, and didn't dare go any faster than five or six miles an hour. At that rate, I wouldn't get home before spring.

The traffic diminished almost to ghost town levels. Apparently, not too many drivers wanted to deal with the snowy mountain. A snow plow had pushed the bulk of the white stuff off the roadway, but nowhere was the black visible. As fast as they pushed the accumulation aside, it accumulated all over again. I was thankful that I didn't have to push new-fallen snow out of my way. Because there was little to no traffic, I risked going up to ten miles per hour. I came close to sliding out a few times, but having done that sort of thing in other snow storms, I was not overly intimidated. Sliding on my hip would leave a bruise, at the worst. Nevertheless, my body was as tight as a banjo string.

To reach the bottom of the Blue Ridge took two hours. The beginning of the mountain is very distinct. Its slope comes with little transition. One might expect a sign saying, "There be bears here." Instead, there was a convenience store. This was a time long before the advent of cell phones, so this was my last chance to make a telephone call from the ubiquitous phone booths that these commercial facilities usually harbored. But who would I call? No! I was in this for the whole ride. This blizzard was not going to get the better of me. I stopped for about ten minutes, unkinking my tensed-up body. My hands were frozen and balled up into a clenched hammer. I'd been gripping the throttle and brakes forever. My feet were blocks of cold concrete. They needed respite and motion. The twenty-four-hour convenience store was closed. I cursed them. I walked around their parking lot stamping blood back into my toes and flexing life and feeling back into my hands. No one had cleared out the parking area, so I had to push through the drifts as I went. Finally, I was ready, sort of. The engine had to be started by cranking the pedals while the bike stood on its stand, because there was not enough traction to roll start it.

As soon as the moped hit the starting slope, I knew I was in trouble. There was not enough traction to go up. Now what was I going to do? There was only one option. I had to walk up the mountain while pushing the bike up the slopes. The engine needed to be running because I needed enough light to see the mountain. Mopeds don't have batteries to make their lights shine. The lights work off the electricity generated by their motors. As I walked, I would have to give the motor enough gas to keep the wheels moving slowly, so that I didn't have to completely muscle it up the entire God-forsaken mountain road.

A snow plow passed me once. He never offered any help. I don't know what he could have done anyway. In a way, I was glad not to humble myself by accepting help. I didn't get a second chance. The plows had gone home for the night. I was the only two-legged, two-wheeled creature stupid enough to be on that mountain at this hour.

Going from downtown Harrisonburg to the top of the mountain, Skyline Drive, took about four hours. There are some monument stones on the crest, as well as an entrance to Skyline Drive. I stopped there to catch my breath and work warmth back into my hands. Everything ached, especially my shoulders and arms. I had just pushed a motorbike up an entire mountain. My core temperature was more than toasty. In fact, I was sweating underneath my winter garb. My hands and arms, however, were aching blocks of ice. It was fifteen minutes before I was willing to face the downward journey. But it was time to head down.

Down is scarier than up. I slid very, very slowly down the steep, curved slopes. My feet acted like outriggers, and both hands clamped the hand brakes constantly. My arms were already exhausted from pushing. Now they had to hold my upper torso off the handlebars. I couldn't just coast, because I needed to run the motor to keep the headlights on. Halfway down, I ran out of gas. It had been a worry in the back of my mind almost the entire journey, but I had managed to keep it at bay. In a way, it was unthinkable.

One good thing about white snow is that it reflects ambient light very nicely. I couldn't determine where the roadside began even when the lights were working. But the road had been plowed hours before, and snow was thicker along the roadside than in the middle. There were several times when I was sure I had gone off the road, however. Despite my visual impairment, I managed not to go off the side of the mountain. I would have noticed that.

There is a relatively flat expanse before the mountain makes its final descent on the eastern side. There are a few nondescript stores on the north side of the highway. I'd never stopped to find out what they were for. But at this point, I'd reached my limit. Even if I succeeded in getting down the mountain, I still would have had twenty miles to go before reaching home. I certainly wasn't going to pedal it. Not on a moped.

I had to get help. Hopefully, those businesses would harbor an outside phone booth or station. I prayed that they did. But who would I call? The Greene County Sheriff's office was a possibility, but only as a last resort. The cops might decide to take me to the fifth floor of the University of Virginia Hospital to check out my sanity.

At that point, I wouldn't have blamed them. I racked my exhausted frozen brain for alternatives. Who could I call in the middle of the night in a blizzard? The whole notion seemed ludicrous.

Then, the name David came to me like a ghost in the flurry that surrounded me. Why David? We weren't close friends. On the other hand, he had a pickup truck. We could load the moped on the truck bed. Why would he come? He was out of work, and I could pay him—a lot. Would he brave the weather? He was a Texan. Of course he would. But would he kill me for getting him up in the middle of the night with such a preposterous proposition? Maybe. Oh hell, I was going to die on this mountain anyway. Nevertheless, I should be ashamed of myself for even thinking of calling him, but I was beyond shame at that point.

There was a phone booth. The simple act of finding change, putting it into the slots, and dialing the operator was a herculean task for my frozen fingers. I dared not drop the coins in the snow. Eventually, I managed to get the operator to find and dial his number.

Never again will I say anything against Texans. David was my hero. He was the equivalent of a Texas Ranger saving an hombre from a band of marauding banditos. He rode in on his stallion within the hour. We loaded the moped on the truck bed, and he drove me home.

Ironically, two miles past the base of the mountain, the roads were dry. No snow! That is not unusual for Virginia. The weather on one side of the mountain is often totally different from the other side.

My dog was waiting for me when we arrived. David accepted payment for his trouble. The amount of money could not possibly have been enough. I remember the hot shower, but I don't remember going to bed.

Ira J. Barron, Tomato Farmer

Joy Merritt Krystosek

(Second place nonfiction, Blue Ridge Writers Chapter contest, VWC, 2017)

Ira J. Barron, died on May 8, 1980. Grandpa was seventy-five-years old when he died, but he sure looked like a hundred. Grandpa had been ill for quite some time, failing kidneys and certainly lung problems from smoking most of his life. During his last days in the hospital, we learned he had been born with only one kidney. Amazing that he lived so long, especially considering the amount of beer he drank. Grandpa was taken to the intensive care unit at the Richmond, Indiana, hospital, where he was kept comfortable for the remaining days before his death. He died holding hands with four of his children after having acknowledged his acceptance of the Lord. That was a great comfort and joy to all of us—knowing he would be with Grandma in heaven.

Grandpa was always a slight man, but sinewy and muscular from many long hours of work on his tomato farm. He was tan beyond a moderate shade of brown; constant exposure to the sun brought many wrinkles to his face and hands. Henceforth, we shall refer to his features as "leathery." He was more than likely not freshly shaven or showered. He worked all day and came in to wash, from the waist up; eat his midday meal; and go back out to finish work. Any part left of the evening was spent in front of the television set with a beer in his hand.

Grandpa was a forerunner for the farmers market. He would pile tables with his garden produce and baskets of tomatoes. He often gave away bushels of his prize tomatoes and other produce to families that could not afford to pay and had nothing to trade. I also remember him being good to the Mexican migrant workers and their families who came each year to work for him. They all liked him and they laughed and joked together. Grandpa seemed to understand them quite well, although I doubt he knew much of the Spanish language. The workers and their families stayed in Quonset huts on the farm. Each night you could hear them playing cards; the only light was one bare light bulb hanging from an electric cord in the ceiling. Grandpa would allow my sister and me to go to the huts and watch them play cards. It was fascinating to see. We understood very little of what they said, but there was always a lot of laughter and an air of kindness.

We played with the migrant workers' small children, the ones who were not working in the fields or doing something to help their parents. There is no language barrier with little kids; you just play. We would get so tan from being out in the sun all day and filthy dirty. Grandpa did not require us to bathe while we were on the farm. I guess he left that up to us. I remember my mom picking us up after a week on the farm. She was furious at him and accused him of not bathing us. Well, that was true. She would take us home and stand us up on the toilet and scrub us with a brush and soap before she would even allow us in the bathtub. She would ask us what we ate while we were on the farm, and we answered, "Just Clark Bars and eggs." She was pretty mad. Another time she came to the farm to pick us up and overheard a lady from town talking about the "grubby little Mexican kids playing in the barnyard." My mom interrupted her and said, "Those are not migrant workers' children; they are my daughters." She stomped over and grabbed us by the overall straps and threw us in the car. My grandpa and my uncle, Dennis, were both doubled over with laughter. Uncle Dennis had an old trailer parked on the farm. The axel was broken, so it listed to one end, so much so that you could not get from one end to the other. My sister and I used to pretend it was our own place. Grandpa allowed us to stay in there as long as we wanted, which wasn't long. The trailer was so tilted that we could only sit at the bench table. It was too steep of a climb to do anything else. But I remember feeling very grown-up at having our own "place."

Ira Barron was not a prejudiced man; he was friends with everyone. I have heard stories that many years before, in Kentucky, he had a black man paroled to him. Bill lived right there in a room in the back of the family home. In the early 1940s that was a bold move. Grandpa always said that Bill was wrongly accused of his crime and should not have gone to prison in the first place.

Grandpa did not ever learn to read or to write. I suppose he had some schooling but quit to help support his family on their farm in Woodstock, Kentucky. He was probably just six or seven years old when he left school. He told me years later that he left home for a few years to work on a riverboat on the Ohio River. He eventually returned to the farm in Kentucky. His lack of reading and writing did not hinder his good business sense. My mom and her sisters had simple invoices made up that could be filled in easily by his customers; no one seemed to mind or make a big deal about it. He could carry on a great conversation when he was in the mood and seemed to have considerable knowledge of politics and what was going on in the world. Grandpa had the nickname "Hawker," I suppose because he hawked his produce at the cannery or in town. I think he must have known his "numbers" well enough to negotiate buying and selling for the farm.

About fifteen years after Grandpa died, I had a conversation with my mom. I was visiting her from where I lived in Florida. She was talking about him like he had just died. I turned to her and said, "Mom, I know you must miss grandpa a lot. I do too. Sometimes I feel like he's looking down at me from Heaven or that he is here with me."

Mom answered me with tears in her eyes, "I grieve for him every day and for my mother; I know they are with me; they never leave me."

* * * *

After I returned to Florida, I had a very poignant experience that confirmed my feelings of my grandpa being with me in spirit and brought back those memories of my time with him. "If you are looking down at me, Grandpa, this story is for you!"

I am heading to Sanford, Florida, for a fun day, all by myself. Sanford is about thirty-five miles from where I live in Orlando, right on the St. John's River. Sanford is a quaint little historic town with lots of bed and breakfasts and shops. The architecture is so different from what you think would be in Florida. Both Sanford and parts of Orlando are full of old houses, with architecture of eras of the past. Many are Mission- and Craftsman-style homes on tree-lined streets. Sure, there are lots of palm trees, but they share the soil with crepe myrtles and northern pines, and massive bushes of bougainvillea. The deep crimson bougainvillea climbs up the side of the house. a wonder to both sight and smell.

Today is a perfect spring day in Florida, a balmy 85 degrees, no humidity, and with enough crosswinds to be *perfect comfort*. I gather up my sketch pad and pencils, pack the car with a blanket, and head northeast.

As I pull into Sanford I see a sweet little bistro near the area I want to go. I get out of my car and head to the Willow Tree for lunch. The Willow Tree is a renovated bait shop near the river. They still have the old graying wood screen door that slams each time someone enters or leaves. The place is somewhere between rustic and faux-nouveau. I notice the girl behind the counter is wearing a name tag, "Chancey." I smile and say, "Hi, Chancey. What a lovely name you have."

"Thanks. Chancey is my mother's family name. Mom wanted it passed on and thought it would be a good idea to give that name to her firstborn. Well, that was me, and here I am!" Chancey is a cute and very perky sixteen-year-old.

I order lunch and a small dessert and ask Chancey, "Can you please put that in a bag or box for me? I'm heading to the river for a picnic."

"Sure thing. Which direction are you going? Don't go on the grassy area by the riverbank; stay up on the concrete, where the high fencing is. There's a few picnic tables and the view of the river is pretty." Chancey seems pretty adamant that I not go to the edge of the riverbank.

I take her advice and head to my picnic *near* the river. My quiet, serene picnic isn't working out so well. Florida has what you call "blind mosquitoes" They don't bite but they sure annoy the hell out of you as they fly at you, landing on your clothes, blanket, in your purse, in your drink, in your mouth, just about anywhere they can. Blind? I don't think so. Seems to me they know just where they're going. To top that off a huge alligator comes within fifty feet of me. Oh sure, he is in the water on the other side of the fence, but he sure looks like he can scale the six-foot wall, the only thing separating us. I need to find a better place for my outing.

I gather up my blanket, lunch bag, and sketch pad and walk two blocks to the center of town. The streets remind me of Midwest small-town life—lots of department stores and antique shoppes, even a corner drug store with a soda fountain. The people seem friendly; they stop to talk to each other on the street as they pass, shouting hellos and greetings to each other. I like this town. I feel really good today. I decide to walk farther and stop in a brick square right in the center of town. The whole street is blocked off from traffic. It appears to be a miniature park, with benches, street lanterns, and lots of trees and bushes. Very quaint—perfect, in fact. This is my spot for today.

I spy an empty bench and spread out my lunch and lay my sketch pad out. People are coming and going. A few even stop to say hello and to ask what I draw.

There's an old black man sitting on the bench across from me. He was here when I arrived two hours ago. He's sitting with a plastic bag on his knees. The bag appears to be papers or envelopes of some kind. Earlier I heard a couple of people say hello to him. He answered them, but in a very timid manner, not making eye contact. He reminds me of my Grandpa Barron. OK, I know my grandpa is not black, but he did have dark, leathery skin and wore his hat just the same way this man wears his.

It's late, and, as I gather up my stuff to leave, I look over at him and smile and say hello. He smiles back and says, "Hello to you, young lady."

I start to walk away and glance over at him. I hesitate because it seems like he wants to ask me something.

I look over at him, and he says, "Young lady, can you help me with something?"

"I sure hope so. What can I do for you?" I put my stuff back down on the bench and walk over to him. He pulls out papers from his plastic bag. They look like invoices or bills.

"Young lady, will you help me with these so I can pay them and get them in the mail?"

"Sure, no problem."

Not knowing exactly what he needs from me, I sit down beside him. "What do you need for me to do for you, sir?"

"Just fill these out for me," he says, very timidly.

I counter with, "OK. Do you have a pen?"

"No pen."

"Well, I only have my drawing pencils and they won't do." I look across the park area and see two ladies chatting on a park bench. I walk over and ask, "Excuse me, do you ladies have a pen we could borrow?"

The first lady, avoiding eye contact with me, says, very curtly, that she has no pen. The second lady searches through her bag and comes up with one. "Keep it," she says, in a very curt tone.

OK, why are they being so rude? Then it hits me. Perhaps they don't approve of my friendly nature with a black man.

I walk back to the man. He hands me two bills and two cashier checks and then points at the different lines on the paperwork. I knew he didn't understand them, so I finished filling them out for him. Something was compelling me to offer to sign his checks for him.

"Would you like for me to go ahead and sign these?" He appears eager and happy with my suggestion. I try to make light of the whole thing and act as though it is perfectly normal. "I do this for my boss all the time; I even forge his signature when he's away and we have to get a report out." We both laugh.

"OK, what name do I put on this?"

With a big smile and a proud tone he says, "John W. White is my name."

I finish his bills, put them in the stamped envelopes, and hand them to John W. White. He bids me a fond farewell and I head to my car. As I walk, it hits me that he doesn't read or write. I think my heart is going to burst open right in the middle of town. What a sight for the fine people of Sanford to witness. Tears stream down my face. I am so grateful that the Lord kept me humble and quiet. I would not want to embarrass or humiliate John W. White. If it weren't for experiencing my grandpa's inability to read or write, I would not have known how to handle it.

Thanks, Grandpa. You *were* here with me. You gave me the instinct and the heart for John W. White.

Stranded

Gerry Kruger

Surrounded by leafy trees and evergreens, wild raspberry bushes, chirping birds, and cool mountain breezes, our only concern was coming face to face with a black bear looking for berries. My best friend, Rob, had persuaded me to take a hike in North Carolina with him to the summit of Mount Mitchell, the highest mountain in the Appalachian chain.

Rob is an adventurous risk taker. He loves skiing, climbing, riding waves at high tide, kayaking, and challenge. I like my feet firmly on level ground and knowing what lies ahead. That said, I still have more fun with Rob than with anyone else. So here I was—climbing the highest mountain in eastern North America, 6,684 feet high.

I was skeptical from the beginning. It was three o'clock in the afternoon before we started. I knew if we hiked up, we'd also have to hike down. This wasn't a mountain we'd want to descend after dark. The sign said, "one and a half miles to the end of the trail," so we decided to ask at the information desk if we could get back before dark. The attendant said we could.

At first it was idyllic. The ascension was gentle and gradual. We joked about beating the bears to the raspberries as we plopped the juicy treats into our mouths. Then the climb grew steeper and the weather cooler. The pleasant early July day was beginning to feel like March. This was no joke.

The worst part of the climb was that huge steppingstones on the trail forced us to jump down from one rocky ledge to another before we could go back up. Going up, then down, then up again made the hike much longer than one and a half miles. As the weather grew chillier, the rocky ledges became slippery. A fall would be treacherous. Soon we began to feel the effects of the changing altitude and were both struggling to breathe.

"Rob, the air smells like snow! How will we get back down if it snows?" I shivered, not having a sweater to wear over my short sleeves and shorts. I was dressed for summer, not winter.

"Maybe we can get a ride back down with somebody at

the top of the trail."

"That man at the information desk should have known better than to tell us we could make it." I'd rather be mad at him than at Rob.

About an hour into our climb, it began to snow. By this time I was sweating and freezing at the same time.

Rob was ahead of me, giving me advice about the best way to tackle the difficult spots. "We should be close to the end of the trail." Rob was trying to encourage me, but he was panting and struggling to keep going.

Tired, cold, and scared that we wouldn't make it to the end, Rob had an idea. "Let's look for the road." We had heard cars passing as we climbed. We could walk on the road to the top instead of climbing rocks and risking a fall.

We soon found the road and in no time came upon a crowd of tourists, vendors, information booths, and a paved parking lot full of cars.

"We made it!" Rob's triumphant cry said it all.

By now it was snowing hard and we were freezing, but we were safe!

"What's that?" Rob was frowning at the construction around the top of the mountain. The road didn't go all the way up.

I wondered if they had closed the final segment of the hike. Rob would be disappointed if he couldn't reach the summit. I was ready for our adventure to end.

He stepped up to the vendor at a nearby booth to inquire about hiking to the top of the mountain.

"It's closed. They're working on the trail," the man said.

Rob shook his head in disbelief. He never liked to leave a task unfinished, and we were within fifty vertical feet of reaching the summit.

"Ask about getting a ride," I whispered.

"Is there anyone who could take us down to our car? We left it at the bottom and hiked up."

The man rolled his eyes and looked at us as if to say, "What fools!"

"Our rangers were out until three o'clock this morning

on search and rescue. We don't have any rides available." His deadpan expression conveyed his lack of sympathy.

"Well, he was helpful," I muttered. "What do we do now?"

"Let's see if somebody will give us a ride. Look, there's a car leaving now." Rob pointed to a car with only two people and ran up to it.

"Do you think you could give us a ride to our car at the bottom of the mountain?"

"I'm sorry, but we're picking up our children over there." The woman pointed to some children getting drinks at one of the booths. There was clearly no room for us.

"There's somebody over there!" I yelled.

Once again we were turned away. The couple said there was no room. Their car was packed with their baggage and gear.

"Do we look untrustworthy?" I didn't think we'd have so much trouble getting a ride. Having to depend on the kindness of strangers was no walk in the park. (Forgive the pun.)

Then we spotted a woman getting into a huge SUV with two very small children.

"Look!" I pointed to the vehicle several yards away.

We both made a mad dash toward the car.

I stepped up this time. "Do you have room enough to take us to our car at the bottom of the mountain!" It was getting dark and snowing hard. I'm sure my desperation was visible.

"Sure, hop on in."

And hop in we did! In minutes we were back at Rob's silver convertible at the foot of the mountain and on our way.

Once again I had survived one of Rob's hair-raising adventures. It wasn't the first and probably won't be the last. In spite of the risks he takes, he usually lands on his feet. If I know Rob, he'll go back and climb those fifty vertical feet to the summit.

ON WRITING AND PUBLISHING

A Eulogy for Fonts

Jody Hobbs Hesler

Before my parents divorced, we lived in a puny little Blue Ridge Mountain town called Berryville, Virginia. If anyone I meet has heard of it, chances are pretty good they drove through it on their way somewhere else. By a slimmer chance, maybe they came across Gunter's Honey, produced by a regional honeyworks that's been in business my whole life. Or, by even slimmer chance, perhaps they partook of a fruitcake from the local monastery. I never imagined that Berryville might produce something important until the day I paged upon a colophon declaring that the very book in my hands had been typeset and printed in Berryville. My tiny little town mattered after all.

Maybe it was during my earliest readings of Jane Austen that I happened upon my first-ever colophon, this one announcing which typeface the book had used. Whenever it was, I was very young, and terribly impressed. Reading that little paean to Garamond, let's say, I was struck by the notion of one art supporting another—a beautiful sort of relationship between typeface and word, something I'd never considered before.

These glorifying little colophons held up the whole procedure of the printing of a book not for inspection but for celebration. *Eureka! This work of art has been accomplished!* And, *Eureka again!* It has been accomplished through meticulous craftsmanship—requiring individuals to manipulate very specific artisanal letters that had been created by artists, or in memory of a particular artist, or in the manner of a particular artist from ages past. These celebrations included the art of the book in my hand as well as generations of art before it.

Now, publishing happens in a series of cloak-and-dagger exchanges of document files or thumb drives, not via printed pages slipped into envelopes and christened with stamps. Journals and book publishers still have style choices, but writers? We must forget the Garamonds and Baskervilles, the Helveticas and Bodonis. Forget the careful typesetters, the artists crafting alphabets. Forget that art exists behind other art at all—because today we writers must use Times New Roman, and only Times New Roman, because it is the *lingua franca*, or the *"fontus" franca*?

But, o, how I loathe Times New Roman!

The font is callous. Its letters are too thick. Their shapes are dull and blighted. I love High Tower Text, Bernhard Modern, Centaur—lean, clean lines with a light, elegant touch. I love fonts in general. I used to match font to atmosphere of story—but too much changeability creates technical issues and appears inconsistent in a body of work.

For a long time, I settled upon Centaur, which I had felt was Times New Roman-ish enough to keep from annoying editors with unnecessary curlicues or unreadable italics or bizarre substitutions for punctuation marks. Much to my chagrin, I learned that this font often transmitted to others as a small caps version of some other font.

Small caps! I was shouting, albeit restrainedly, entire stories at editors. God bless them for answering me at all. I must have seemed amateurish, just because I had hoped to escape the stranglehold of Times New Roman—a print style that stubs the sharpness of letters, squashes their heights, and above all conforms every story to the same beautyless condition.

Perhaps Times New Roman, at its debut, was a thing of beauty. Perhaps a story set in Times New Roman once even caught my eye, driving me to search for those endpages of whatever edition I might have been reading, hoping to learn the secret of the artistry behind the loveliness of the letters on the page. But there is no joy left in Times New Roman today.

Now, against my own desires, I draft stories, essays, articles, book reviews, novels, all in this drudgery of a font. On my stale days, when the work is slow, the font as much as shrugs its shoulders at me. It's a bystander—apathetic and disengaged. Never does it shout *Eureka!* Or *Hark! A work of art is underway!*

I know that's my job: to make the work of art proclaim itself. But can you blame me for being drawn to the old way—of art holding hands with other art, supporting it, celebrating it, sharing it?

As writers, we do so much of everything alone. Dear fonts, I miss you so.

When Words Fight

Lauvonda Lynn Young

My Poem arose as nighttime on the
mountain, was morphing into a delightful day
in the dark, my Poem, let Words have their say
although, no accomplished rhyme, was birthed
After sustenance, my Poem set about
to finalize, a stupendous work of art
sleeping Words, spiteful, were ripped apart
reordered without thought, or kindness
Some Words fought a reshuffle, on lined paper
others wanted to play, as the weather was fine
my Poem thought this, a full-fledged crime
reviled he felt, believed his verse, was cursed
Alas, I could not, dive in and help
since my pen, was void of ink
all the Words died, made a huge stink
my Poem, sought a shrink, next day

Give 'Em What They Want

Michael McLeod

(Third place nonfiction, Blue Ridge Writers Chapter contest, VWC, 2017)

Occasionally I get requests from friends and acquaintances to tell them how wonderful their just-finished manuscript is. They don't actually say, "Tell me it's wonderful," but that's what they expect to hear. Most of the time I can't do that, partly because at one time I was a professional reader.

Professional reader? Yes, young Jedi, there are people in this world who get paid to read your manuscript. A reader evaluates your submission and writes a short report for the big boss. Bosses are way too busy to read the stuff in the slush pile. Their job is to sell manuscripts that they already know are marketable.

Readers are people with no power. Even if they believe that your manuscript is the best thing they've ever read, they have no power to get it published or produced. All they can do is pass it further up the ladder, along with a positive review.

However, "no power" is a double-edged sword. The other edge is the ability to say, "No." When that happens, you're dead. Your immortal prose will not go up the ladder.

Few people make a career out of being a professional reader. Most readers are struggling writers, many with degrees in literature, English, or specific types of writing such as film and television or children's literature. They are trying to pay the bills while they work on their own masterpiece. And paying the bills isn't easy, because professional readers do not make big bucks. Most readers do it to get a foot in the door or because they want to learn what it takes to get their own manuscript past a pro reader.

A professional reader can tell in a few seconds whether a submission is worth reading, without reading a single word. How is that possible? Format.

The reader picks up a submission and riffles the pages from back to front. From that simple act, they can get a good idea about whether you know what you're doing. How? What is the reader looking for? Wrong font, incorrect line spacing, headers and footers incorrect, the overall format is not correct for the genre in which you are submitting . . . (narrative fiction is different from film, which is different from TV, which is different from a children's picture book, which is different from . . .), and so forth.

The reader wants your submission to be good. In fact, they want it to be great. They want to discover the next big success. But day after day they read stuff submitted by people who fail to demonstrate that they understand fundamental writing craftsmanship. So, when the back-to-front riffle test fails, the reader's hopes are dashed. They will still read the submission, because that's what they are paid to do. But now, instead of looking forward to it, they are dreading what is to come. Frankly, from that point on, you'd have to be Faulkner or Hemingway to get past this reader.

Let's assume that our hypothetical reader works for a hypothetical agent who represents writers of material intended for children and young adults. A glance at the title of your submission (*Sex in the Bronx*) lowers the reader's expectations another notch. Didn't this submitter do basic research about what the agency wants? Obviously not. Strike two.

In reality, if you submitted *Sex in the Bronx* to this particular agent, it would probably get rejected by a secretary rather than being assigned to a reader. When a submission is so obviously wrong for an agency or publication, they don't need to pay a reader to tell them that.

However, in our hypothetical situation, it did get assigned, so the reader opens the submission to the first page and begins reading. By the end of the second page, she has found four punctuation errors, three misplaced modifiers, and two misspelled words. Strike three.

The reader has no idea whether the submission is properly structured, or entertaining, or at least interesting. She knows nothing about the wonderful, heartwarming story that is buried inside. And she could not care less.

There are plenty of things that will get you a polite rejection, even after you get past the professional reader. But you do have to get past the reader first. It is your responsibility to make the reader's job as easy and enjoyable as possible. You should:

1. Understand what type of content your potential agent or publisher is seeking: *Writer's Market* is a good place to start.

2. Read the publication's submission guidelines, which are almost always available online. In addition to learning the desired length of submissions, you will find out if the publication requires a particular format. You will also determine who should receive your submission. Sending a submission to the wrong person or the wrong department (large publications often have more than one submission editor) is a tip-off that you haven't read their submission guidelines and therefore don't really know what they are looking for.

3. Submit in the correct format for the genre, including font, indents, line spacing, element placement on the page, and so forth. (Google manuscript format). Pay particular attention to submission length. Screenplays that are over or under a narrow page-length allowance are usually automatically rejected. The same applies to children's picture books and other genres.

4. Proofread, proofread, and then proofread again. Then have your friends proofread it. *The Elements of Style* should always be within reach when you are writing. Don't trust your spelling checker: I once found, on a single page, "specious" for "spacious" and "price" for "prize."

If you have good storytelling skills, some agents and publishers are willing to take you in hand and help you improve those skills. Virtually none of them are ready to teach you how to format your document, how to spell, or when to use a period instead of a question mark.

Get the basics down, and you'll get over the first hurdle.

Life in Written Memory

Gary D. Kessler

(Disclaimer: This essay isn't really about painting Christmas cards. It's an urging for writers—and everyone else—to write of their memories and the influences that have made them tick to live on with those they will leave behind. This essay originally was published in *Of Me I Muse*.)

I paint the family Christmas cards, each one individually, using heavy watercolors and the Chinese brush painting style on rice paper that I cut into form and print myself. They generally are simplistic and not major art, but I've taken the time to create each one individually. I've done that for thirty-nine years now, and for years I've made upwards of 120 cards, starting sometimes as early as the previous Christmas. A few years ago I noticed I had a few left over—before that I invariably had to go back into production in December because I hadn't made enough. And then, in succeeding years, I had even more left over. When I realized the need was dwindling and I had cards left over I cut back to making 110 cards. This past year I made 105. I still had a few left over when they all had been sent.

Our friends are dying off faster than we are adding new ones. It's an undeniable sign of creeping mortality.

I sometimes wake up in a sweat at the thought of the inevitable "nothingness" stealing up on me. I've tried believing in a cushy afterlife, one where I can meet up with all those who went before (although I have to agree with my mother's frequent comment that she didn't want to meet up ever again with some of the people she once knew) and look down on how the ones I've left behind are faring, but I just can't pretend to believe what I don't. (Well, I suppose I could and sometimes do—but the older I get the more I resist doing so.)

I admired my mother for years for convincingly saying this fear didn't grip her. She had actually (clinically) died at age nineteen from a botched appendix operation by a drunken rural doctor. Her body had been wheeled out into the corridor for removal the next day. The next morning she was "alive again." Not having sewn her back up had saved her life, permitting the wound to drain.

My mother wasn't the supernatural type of person. But she described having the typical out-of-body experience while judged dead, including the floating feeling, the bright lights, the distant choir, the clouds, and the sensation of sitting on a fence and not really caring which direction she fell on. I pretty much think this is your body's way of smoothing over your transition from life to death and that you weren't truly dead for that part of the experience. But that's just my opinion. My mother didn't disagree with me and she didn't proselytize about this after-life experience; she just used it as a comfort. I'm glad it comforted her for many years, because when she moved toward death, she fought it off like hell for some time and then, when I think she truly welcomed it, the hospital didn't let her go for five months.

I think I'm with the crowd who wants to just keel over unexpectedly when I'm having a great night out on the town.

I have to believe that it isn't in the body or the consciousness that someone can live on past death, but that it only is in the DNA and memories they leave behind. When I look at my children and granddaughters, I can see flashes of my parents and the only grandparent I knew. My (truly) saintly mother-in-law passed on at 102. But she isn't completely gone, because I hear her when my wife laughs and see her when my wife smiles. The amazing thing to me is that I can see traits of my ancestors in grandchildren and grandnieces- and nephews even though they never met and lived in different spans of time.

There isn't anything I can do about DNA, but there is something I can attempt to do about memory retention. I can write of my life influences and memories to pass on to those who follow me (which I recently did in the memory book *Of Me I Muse*) and I can urge others to do the same (hence, this essay).

I came to the realization I think I have about death being conquered by memory nearly too late in life. I was letting memories pass away. Recognizing that this was happening and discussing this with my mother prompted her to make a trip to my paternal grandmother's side when she was in her nineties with a recorder to grasp what she could of that remarkable woman's life. This history has been transcribed for family reunions and is often reflected in prose and poetry in my own writing. Subsequently, my mother did a recording on her own life, which have enriched my writing as well. Without the recordings my grandmother and mother did, bits and pieces of what I already knew about them and of their lives and times probably never would have fit in place. My own children and their children down through time certainly would never know these direct connections with their ancestors.

I don't look on the approach of death—which I trust and fear is a "nothingness" in body and consciousness—by swinging a welcome sign any more than most everyone else does. But I find that my enthusiasm for places and contexts in which I have known special people no longer with us diminishes now that they aren't there. A church I went to for thirty-five years no long has pull now that favorite friends from there—a Quaker federal judge and a brilliant and witty Southern Railroad executive—are gone. I'm even losing hope that the railroad executive's wife, with the beautiful lilting soprano voice, may not outlive me to sing "Wild, Lone Bird" at my funeral. My vivacious sometimes tennis partner and partner-in-crime on theater production in various parts of the world has left me behind, neglecting to tell me how sick she was but thoughtful enough to assign someone to tell me she was gone. The tragedy is that, although she led a fascinating life, she, who was raised backstage at the Met; who renovated a castle on the Hudson River, a process that was followed in a series *New York Time*s feature articles; and who had served as the female U.S. consul general in Saudi Arabia during the first Iraq war, left no accounts of this life behind her—and, more tragically, was the last of her family. The generation of family before me has bowed out. Key people I respected in my current church are no longer here.

I have fewer and fewer Christmas cards to make every year. Sooner than later, I won't be around to paint the cards either. The thought is there to just stop painting them now. But that would be a copout, I think (well, until I reach a round number of years, like forty). While I'm going through the Christmas card creation process, I can still think about those I no longer have a reason to make a card for to send in the flesh, and by bringing up memories of them and being with them even for a few brief moments, I send a different kind of greeting in a different way.

As long as they are in my memory, they aren't dead. And as long as there are those to read my own memories in the form I record them—in words in essays, short stories, and poems rather than recording—I have to believe I won't be dead either to the generations coming on behind me. And if this isn't so, well, oh well, I tried. No harm for trying. Thank goodness for the art of writing and that I enjoy writing and have vehicles for preserving what I write—and so, as writers and readers and as people who have walked this earth and who have family and friends walking behind you, do you.

ABOUT THE AUTHORS

David Black ("Winter Morning, -13," "Country Neighbors," "The Drunk in the Middle of the Night," "The Woodbugger," and "Night Game on Long Mountain," poetry), a retired English teacher and minister, is a former poetry editor of the *English Journal* and a frequent contributor of poems, essays, articles, and reviews to small magazines and academic journals, especially in the Appalachian region. He is the author of three books: *Some Task, Long Forgotten and Other Poems*, *The Clown in the Tent*, and *Shortcomings: Around the Grounds & Corner*.

Stephen Bush (*Skyline* publisher; BRWC contest nonfiction judge; "Vendimia in the Ribeira Sacra in Galicia," nonfiction), born in Singapore and an Australian citizen, now lives in southern Europe. He is the publisher for Cyberworld Publishing, is volume editor for the annual *The Good Life in Galicia* anthology; the author of the novel, *My Sister's Funeral*; short story writer; and author of dog care and grooming manuals. He has run workshops on dog grooming, served as an Australian dog show judge, and raises Chinese Cresteds. Prior to moving to Europe, he lived on the east coast of Australia and for some years in Darwin. He has traveled extensively in northern Australia, where he worked as an accountant. He currently is restoring village houses and resurrecting a vineyard in Spain.

Carol G. Cutler ("Two of the Night," poetry) lives in Albemarle County and writes fiction, nonfiction, and poetry. She participates in several writing groups in the area, including a critique group of the Blue Ridge Writers Chapter of the Virginia Writers Club. Her publications include clinical research in psychiatric nursing, a contributing chapter to a book related to the theology of Paul Tillich, and an essay in *Skyline 2017*. Two poems will appear in the Virginia Writers Club 100th Anniversary Anthology of 2018. Science, nature, and the environment; various social justice issues; and grandchildren are favorite writing topics.

Wendi Dass ("Team Leader," fiction) is an emerging writer from central Virginia. Her short stories have been published in several small literary journals, and she is currently seeking representation for her women's fiction novels. When she's not writing, Wendi can be found wrangling her toddler or devising deceptively delicious problems for her math students.

Phyllis A. Duncan ("A Terrible Beauty," fiction) is a retired bureaucrat but one with an overactive imagination—at least that's what everyone has told her since she first started making up stories in elementary school, prompted by her weekly list of spelling words. A commercial pilot and former FAA safety official, she lives and writes in the beautiful Shenandoah Valley of Virginia. A graduate of Madison College (now James Madison University), she has degrees in history and political science. Her love of politics continues to this day. Her fiction has appeared in numerous literary journals and anthologies. When not writing, reading, reviewing books, singing, watching the Yankees, or cheering on Dale Earnhardt, Jr., she takes delight in spoiling her grandchildren. She is the current president of the Virginia Writers Club.

Stanley A. Galloway ("Chasing," "Winter, 1820," "Proteus' Lament," and "Holiday Rain, with Solo Oboe," poetry) teaches at Bridgewater College in Virginia's Shenandoah Valley. His poetry includes *Just Married* and three chapbooks. His reviews of poetry have been published in such places as *New Orleans Review, Callaloo,* and *Paterson Literary Review*. His book of literary criticism is *The Teenage Tarzan*. He is founder and host of the Bridgewater International Poetry Festival.

Cathy Herbert ("Threads," fiction) is based in Luray, Virginia. Her short stories and essays have been published in *The Delmarva Review, The Kelsey Review, Verse, Truthout,* and the *Lascaux Review,* among others. She has worked as a senior editor for national magazines and as a staff writer for Rodale Press.

Jody Hobbs Hesler ("A Trip to Abilene," fiction; "A Eulogy for Fonts," nonfiction) lives and writes in the foothills of the Blue Ridge Mountains. Her fiction, feature articles, essays, and book reviews appear or are forthcoming in *Gargoyle, Raleigh Review, The Georgia Review, Streetlight Magazine, Sequestrum, South85, [PANK], Steel Toe Review, Valparaiso Fiction Review, Prime Number, Pearl, Potato Eyes Journal, A Short Ride: Remembering Barry Hannah* (VOX Press), *Charlottesville Family Magazine, Charlottesville Wine & Country Living,* and other places. Several of her stories have won regional contests, including the Virginia Writers Club Golden Nib and UVA's Writer's Eye, and appear in prize anthologies. She holds an MFA in fiction from Lesley University.

Sarah Collins Honenberger (*Skyline* and BRWC fiction judge; "Son of Crown of Thorns" and "The Genealogy of Secrets," fiction). Sarah's novel, *Catcher, Caught,* is a Pen/Faulkner Foundation selection in its Writers in Schools program. Audio, German, and Korean editions have been released. With numerous short fiction awards and a fellowship from the Virginia Creative Arts Center, she appears regularly on literary panels and at book festivals. Her other novels include *Minding Henry Lewis* (2014), *Waltzing Cowboys* (2009), and *White Lies: A Tale of Babies, Vaccines and Deception* (2006).

Gary D. Kessler (*Skyline* and BRWC contests coordinator, "A Question of Wisdom," fiction; "Life in Written Memory," nonfiction) is a former CIA analyst, news agency managing editor, diplomat, newspaper columnist, theater critic, movie consultant, book editor, and publishing consultant. His published works include the short story collections *On the Downtown Mall* and *Shadow of the Blue Ridge*; volume editor for the two-volume *WritersNet Anthology of Prose and Poetry* and the four-volume *Blue Ridge Anthology*; coauthor of a publishing reference, *Finding Go! Matching Questions and Resources in Getting Published* and of a Bible study, *(Re)Tell Me the Stories*; author of a mystery novel, *What the Spider Saw*; and author of the memory book *Of Me I Muse.* He has won or placed in multiple Virginia Writers Club annual contests and three times in the UVa Art Museum's Writer's Eye prose contest and took third place in the John Gresham–judged *The HooK* short story contest in

2011. His poetry has appeared in the *Piedmont Virginian*. He also writes pen name mystery novellas and novels.

Gerry Kruger ("Stranded," nonfiction), a native Virginian, moved in 1979 from Richmond to the Charlottesville area. She taught English for twenty-seven years at Charlottesville High School. Since 2004 she has participated as a judge in the Writer's Eye contest, sponsored by the University of Virginia's Fralin Museum of Art. As an essayist on National Public Radio, she detailed the adventures of a lame Canada goose that arrived at her pond on foot in 2000 and stayed with her for nine years. Her first book, *On Kruger Pond: Charlie's Story*, chronicles her unique relationship with this goose and his struggles and triumphs. Gerry hopes to publish another book, which will contain Charlie's story as well as more recent essays about Charlie's descendants that continue to visit the place where they were hatched. Ultimately, she hopes to record all of the essays for the blind.

Joy Merritt Krystosek ("Sister Florence Myrtle Barron," poetry; "Ira J. Barron, Tomato Farmer," nonfiction) lives in Madison County. Joy is the published author of two cookbooks, *Cooking Chicken with Joy* and *Cooking Savory Comfort Foods with Joy*. She is in the process of publishing *The Life and Death of Jacques Albèrt Rainelle,* an interactive adult historical fiction and art book. Joy and three other writers in Lonesome Mountain Prose Writers Group published a collection of their work in 2014 titled *We Grew Wings and Flew*. Her poem, "Grace Merritt," was published in *Skyline 2017* for winning third place in the Virginia Writers Club Blue Ridge Writers Chapter 2017 writing contest. Joy is a member of the Blue Ridge Writers Chapter, the Virginia Writers Club, Lonesome Mountain Prose Writers Group, and WriterHouse.

Susan M. Lanterman ("A Christmas to Remember," nonfiction) writes human-interest stories for the "Commentary" section of Charlottesville's *The Daily Progress* newspaper; is writing a collection of short stories entitled, "Good Night Already: Stories from a Reluctant Innkeeper," based on her Charlottesville B&B; and has written a young adult novel, *Hasta Luego, Santa Claus*, which follows the antics of a teenager and his family of illegal immigrants.

Michael McLeod ("Winter Dance: A Shepherd's Lament," poetry; "Give 'Em What They Want," nonfiction) has been a professional writer for more than forty years. He has worked as an advertising copywriter, a newspaper journalist, a senior staff writer for a Fortune 500 company, and as a story analyst for NBC Entertainment. He is the author of three feature-length screenplays, a TV pilot, five stage productions, numerous short stories, and poetry. An avid student, he has taken advanced writing classes at the American Film Institute and in the University of California system, including UCLA, UCSB, UCSD, and UCI. Michael and his wife recently moved to rural Virginia after more than fifty years in Southern California.

Sigrid Mirabella ("Walking the Mount into Darknesses," poetry), originally from Long Island, New York, defines herself as a social hermit and hopeful skeptic living in rural uncertainty. Her works have won awards and have appeared in *The Blue Ridge Anthology, Mid-America Poetry Review, Skyline, prose and poetry, Long Island Pet Gazette, Lynchburg News and Advance, Dog Fancy, Woman's Day, Countryside, People Magazines*, and various Macmillan/Howell books. In her other life, she works for a humane society in Nelson County, Virginia.

BAMorris ("April 5, 2010, on the Skyline Drive," poetry) is a retired teacher. She lives with her husband in Central Virginia. She began creating stories as a child. She writes short stories, memoirs, essays, and poetry.

Gwendolyn Thompson Poole ("Journey's End," fiction) enjoys creating fictional characters for stories and plays set to the backdrop of slavery and the Civil War, particularly in the Shenandoah Valley area of Virginia. One of her most rewarding writing achievements was her play, *The One Called Peter*, commissioned by the Oliver Community Center in Winchester, Kentucky. This dramatic piece was an adaptation of the life and times of former Kentucky slave, Peter Bruner. She recently won recognition from the Blue Ridge Writers Chapter of the Virginia Writers Club for her story "If God Gave Me Wings." Gwendolyn was born in Lexington, Virginia, but currently resides in Greensboro, North Carolina.

Deborah M. Prum ("Finding Canaan" and "Blank as the Minute After Death," fiction) is the author of *Fatty in the Back Seat* (a young adult novel), *First Kiss and Other Cautionary Tales* (an audiobook collection of humorous essays that first aired on NPR-member stations), *Czars and Czarinas* (an anecdotal and interactive history in iBook format) and *Rats, Bulls and Flying Machines* (a print book about the Renaissance). Her award-winning short fiction has been published in many places, including *The Virginia Quarterly Review*, *The Blue Ridge Anthology*, *Across the Margin*, and *The Sweetbay Review*. Her humorous essays appear in many places, including the *Washington Post* and Charlottesville's *Daily Progress*, and air on NPR-member stations. Her work can be seen at www.deborahprum.com.

Elizabeth Doyle Solomon ("Give Me Once More, My Southland," "Mountain Storm," "Shenandoah Mountains Easter," "Strong Words for Harsh Times," and "Dominion's Planned Destruction," poetry; "Midnight Mountain Birth," nonfiction), a New Orleans native and retired teacher, began writing at age eleven and publishing at age thirteen. Now in her seventies, she reckons her poems total over 60,000. Elizabeth has published two poetry collections, *Seasons* and *The Steering Wheel Poems*, written newspaper columns, and founded the *Central Virginia Leader* newspaper. Her recent awards for both poetry and prose have come from the Poetry Society of Virginia, the Blue Ridge Writers, and the *Skyline* anthology. Until recently, Elizabeth led the Blue Ridge poets' critique group in her home, every Friday, for fourteen years. She is working on her third book, a collection of poems and short stories, *Journey West and Everywhere*.

Olivia Stowe (*Skyline* volume editor; "Hollow Night," fiction) lives and writes in Central Virginia. Stowe's specialty is cozy mystery novellas, which include a thus-far ten-volume series of Charlotte Diamond mysteries, the most recent of which was *Fowler's Folly*. The Christmas season short stories, "Cassandra's Last Spotlight," "Blessedly Cursed Christmas," and "Jesus Speaks Galician" add to this series. She also is the author of the inspirational Savannah novella series. Stowe's standalone mysteries include *Fiddler's Rest*, *Restoration of the Castle*, and *Final Flight*. Her inspirational Christmas short story collections are available in the *Spirit of Christmas* and *Christmas Seconds* anthologies. This is the fifth annual volume of *Skyline* she has volume edited in conjunction with Cyberworld Publishing.

Roger Tolle ("First Dance," nonfiction). After years as a professional modern dancer in Boston and New York City, Roger Tolle built a thriving practice in Trager Movement Education. His writing about this work was published in the *Massage Therapy Journal*, Melbourne's *NOW!* magazine, and in the videos and body reminder cards on his website, www.RogerTolle.net. He currently teaches professional training and personal growth workshops around the world and works as a Surrogate Partner for men going through sex, intimacy, and relationship therapy. He writes and travels from his base in Charlottesville, Virginia.

Jack Trammell ("Call of the North," poetry; "We the People (The Fourth Branch of Government)," nonfiction) is an award-winning author and poet, whose credits include hundreds of articles and stories and more than twenty books. He was a recent candidate for U.S. Congress in representative Eric Cantor's seat and has enjoyed a twenty-five-year career as an educator in the public schools and as a professor and researcher in higher education. His areas of expertise include social history, disability education, government, American history, and creative writing. He was a long-time columnist for the *Washington Times*. His recent book projects include *The Fourth Branch of Government: We the People*, coauthored with Guy Terrell, a forthcoming history of disability in America, and a recently released historical Civil War novella. He can be reached at jacktrammell@yahoo.com.

Leonard Tuchyner ("Over the Snowy Blue Ridge on a Moped at Night," nonfiction) is a semiretired counselor, living in Central Virginia with his wife of thirty-eight years and two dogs. He maintains an active involvement in the local writing community, which includes participation in a writing critique group and in the Blue Ridge Writers Chapter of the Virginia Writers Club. Although challenged by legal blindness, he continues to pursue Tai Chi and related forms of martial arts. Gardening is another passion that has captivated him for most of his seventy-seven-year life. One of his most fulfilling endeavors is the facilitation of a Senior Center's Writing for Healing and Growth writing group. He has been in the winners' circle of the VWC Blue Ridge Writer Chapter's yearly writing contest several times. His winning entries have included poetry, fiction, and nonfiction. He has also been a regular contributor to *The Blue Ridge Anthology*. Mr. Tuchyner has published essays, poetry, and short stories in *Dialogue Magazine* (for which he is a columnist), *Magnets and Ladders*, *Nomad's Choir*, *Westward Quarterly*, and *Skyline*. A poetry book, *A Journey to Elsewhere*, was published in 2014.

Erin Newton Wells ("What You Need to Know About the Mountain" and "If a Tree Falls," fiction, and "Night Tune," "Variations on the Annual Theme," "My Face an Elegy," "Not Only Charleston," "The Hunter," "A Glory Around You," and "My Grandmother's Bowl and Pitcher," poetry) writes in several genres, concentrating on poetry. She has won many awards through the Poetry Society of Virginia and was awarded first prize for poetry, 2017, in the Writer's Eye contest, sponsored by the Fralin Museum. Her writing appears in *Poetry South*, *Poetry Virginia Review*, *Spillway*, *The Sow's Ear Poetry Review*, *The Writer's Eye*, and *Skyline*, among others. Her work will also be represented in the three categories of fiction, nonfiction, and poetry in the forthcoming *The Best of Virginia Writers Club: Centennial Anthology, 1918–2018*.

Valerie B. Williams ("The Succession," fiction) has been writing fiction for six years. She is a member of the Virginia Writers Club and the Horror Writers Association (HWA). She is participating in the 2017 HWA Mentorship program, working with Bram Stoker Award–winning author, Tim Waggoner. Valerie has had three essays published in a local Maryland newspaper. She has focused on short stories while honing her craft, and is currently working on her first novel. Her fiction is not always in the horror genre, but tends to be dark. Valerie lives outside of Charlottesville, Virginia, with her very patient husband and two equally patient Golden Retrievers.

Lauvonda Lynn Young ("Challenge" and "When Words Fight," poetry), author of the poetry collection *Just a Woman*, writes in various genres, including poetry, fiction, nonfiction, and memoir (mostly fact based). She has been published in anthologies, newspapers, magazines, and other sources. Lynn plans, organizes, moderates, and presents programs and workshops. In June 2017, Lynn presented a morning and afternoon workshop (Topic: Query Letters), for the Appalachian Authors Guild, Virginia Writers Club (Abington, Virginia), and a workshop (Topic: Self-Publishing) for the Skyline Writers Club (Luray, Virginia) in July 2017. In addition, Lynn was the guest speaker for the July 2017 monthly meeting of the Appalachian Authors Guild (VWC). Lynn served as a member of the Executive Committee of the Poetry Society of Virginia for many years and was the program chair for the annual poetry contest and annual awards ceremony in 2014 and 2016. Past president of the Blue Ridge Writers Chapter, Virginia Writers Club, Lynn received the VWC Superior Service Award in 2011. Lynn also served as secretary and newsletter editor for the BRWC, VWC. She holds memberships in the Appalachian Authors Guild, the Blue Ridge Writers Chapter of the VWC, the James River Writers, and the Poetry Society of Virginia.

Nicole Yurcaba ("Kenova," poetry) is an instructor in the Bridgewater College English Department in Bridgewater, Virginia. She is the author of *Hollow Bottles* (2016) and the forthcoming novel *Razorblade Kyiv* (2017).

Skyline 2017

The fourth collection of works by
Central Virginia Writers

Skyline 2017

Olivia Stowe, ed.

Prose and Poetry
by Central Virginia Writers

Skyline 2016

The third collection of works by Central Virginia Writers.

Skyline 2016

Olivia Stowe, ed.

Prose and Poetry
by Central Virginia Writers

Skyline 2015

The second collection of works by Central Virginia Writers.

Skyline 2014

The first collection of works by Central Virginia Writers.

Skyline 2014

Olivia Stowe, ed.

Prose and Poetry by Central Virginia Writers